Queen Elizabeth
THE QUEEN
MOTHER

Nicholas Courtney

Salem House
Salem, New Hampshire

First published in the United States by
Salem House, 1984. A Member of the Merrimack
Publishers' Circle, 47 Pelham Road, Salem, N.H. 03079

This book was designed and produced by
The Rainbird Publishing Group Ltd,
40 Park Street, London W1Y 4DE

Library of Congress Catalog
Card Number: 84-051781

ISBN 0-88162-026-2

Text set by SX Composing Ltd, Rayleigh, Essex, England
Colour originated by Gilchrist Bros. Ltd, Leeds, England
Printed and bound by Henri Proost & Cie PVRA, Turnhout, Belgium

Acknowledgments

The publishers would like to thank the following for permission to reproduce illustrations:

Reproduced by Gracious Permission of Her Majesty the Queen: 71 and 79; Reproduced by Gracious Permission of Her Majesty Queen Elizabeth the Queen Mother: 3, 21, 48, 54, 84, 91; Crown copyright, By permission of the Controller of Her Majesty's Stationery Office: 78 (right); Alpha/Jim Bennett: 122 (left); BBC Hulton Picture Library: 38 (left), 40 (left), 42 (left and right), 47, 50, 85 (left), 93 (above), 95, 96, 97, 100, 101 (above), 107 (left), 112, 114, 116; The Honourable Lady Bowes-Lyon (photos: Derrick Witty): 18, 19, 27 (right), 33, 69 (right); Camera Press: Frontispiece/Norman Parkinson, 2/Norman Parkinson, 7/Norman Parkinson, 23/ILN, 75, 104/Baron, 105/Baron, 109/John Scott, 113 (right)/Cecil Beaton, 121/Buckley, 125/Norman Parkinson; Country Life Books: 6, 13, 14, 51, 61 (right); Tim Graham: 9, 11, 108, 123, 126 (right), 127; Anwar Hussein: 122 (right); The Illustrated London News: 37, 38 (right), 41, 58, 59, 66 (left), 76 (both)/Derrick Witty, 77, 78 (left), 80/Derrick Witty, 82; Keystone Press Agency: 40 (right), 61 (left), 62 (right), 68, 83, 88, 92, 94, 99, 119, 124; The Mansell Collection: 24, 30 (left), 36, 46; National Portrait Gallery, London: 49 (both); Photographers International: 117, 126 (left)/Terry Fincher; The Press Association Limited: 12, 45 (above), 55, 110 (left), 128; Popperfoto: 22, 25, 29, 30 (right), 31 (right), 32, 34, 35, 45 (below), 52, 53 (left), 60, 62 (left), 63, 64, 69 (left), 70, 72 (above), 73, 80 (right), 85 (right), 86 (above), 89, 90, 98 (below), 102, 103, 107 (right), 110 (right), 113 (left), 118; S & G Press Agency Limited: 98 (above); Syndication International: 15, 26, 31 (above), 42 (below), 44, 53 (right and below), 65, 81, 111, 120; Times Newspapers Limited: 74, 101 (below); Topham: 20, 27 (left), 28, 31 (left), 39 (left and right), 72 (below), 86 (left), 93 (below), 115; Gerd Treuhaft: 66 (right), 105 (below), 106; Woodmansterne Limited/Jeremy Marks: 17

Contents

Introduction

On the desk of Queen Elizabeth the Queen Mother's home stands a beautiful gilt and crystal screen, designed like a triptych. Its central panel is the exact size for a piece of Clarence House writing paper. Major Tom Harvey commissioned the artist Laurence Whistler to make the screen as a present for the Queen Mother on his departure from her service after many happy and devoted years as her Private Secretary. On the side panels are engraved two verses, the right commemorating DUTIES, the left, PLEASURES, while the centre holds a piece of paper typed up with the day's engagements. Under the verses are engraved apposite symbols; for Duties there are a microphone (broadcasts), a mortarboard (her interest in university life as a Chancellor at London and Dundee), a military drum (for the many regiments whose Colonel-in-Chief she is), scissors (for cutting tapes), a trowel (for laying foundation stones) and a key (to the many Freedoms of Cities conferred on her around the world) – all symbols of her busy public life – and, at the very bottom, a car leaving Buckingham Palace. On the other side, under Pleasures, are a landing net (for fishing), binoculars (for racing), musical instruments and the mask of a Terpsichore and, below, an Ascot landau at Ascot Racecourse. It was an imaginative present, for it illustrated the main activities of the Queen Mother as well as being useful. However, it is not totally representative in one respect as the design separates duties from pleasures; and to the Queen Mother these are, and always have been, one and the same thing. The cyphers on the triptych tell only part of the story of the Queen Mother for, as she herself has said, she

Queen Elizabeth the Queen Mother at her desk at Clarence House, her London home

has 'always been helped and uplifted by the love of my family, the loyalty and understanding of our people and by my faith in Almighty God'.

The Queen Mother is the head of her immediate family. This is not solely through age as the surviving member of her generation, nor her unique position as the daughter-in-law, the sister-in-law and the Queen Consort of three successive sovereigns and the mother of Queen Elizabeth II,

The Queen Mother with her daughters – a portrait taken by Norman Parkinson on the occasion of her eightieth birthday on 4 August 1980

but through the love that she gives to and inspires from her large family. The Prince of Wales freely admits to being partisan where his grandmother is concerned. He spoke for the whole family when he wrote, 'She has been the most wonderful example of fun, laughter, warmth, infinite security. . . . She belongs to that priceless brand of human beings whose greatest gift is to enhance the life of others through her own effervescent enthusiasm for life.' Not unnaturally, her immediate family, the Queen and Princess Margaret and their children, come first in her affections. Even in the most difficult times she made a loving home for her

daughters, just as she herself had had as a child. Today, mother and daughters are just as close. The Queen Mother telephones the Queen every day; a senior telephone operator at Buckingham Palace admits that her favourite moment of the day is putting one through to the other, 'Your Majesty? Her Majesty, Your Majesty!' The Queen Mother is fiercely loyal to all her family – when Princess Margaret was under attack in the press over her marriage plans and, later on, her divorce, the Queen Mother made a point of being seen with her as often as possible publicly, quite apart from the support she gave in private. She dotes on her six grandchildren and four great-grand-children as well as her dozens of nephews and nieces, now in their second and third generations. She is particularly fond of the Prince of Wales, her first grandson. 'He's a darling,' she has said. She can see in him many of the qualities of her late husband, while he is indeed fortunate to have inherited so many of hers. Princess Anne has been heard to say that she was depressed that she could never match her grandmother on any level, but where courage and dedication are concerned, she has recently shown that she is not far behind, with her recent tours of Africa and a visit to war-torn Beirut, visiting the projects of her favourite charity, The Save the Children Fund.

It is not only her family who dote on the Queen Mother; she is everybody's 'Queen Mum', the 'granny' that young and old alike would love to have. She is just one lovable person – the Royal Family's own grandmother is exactly the same person the public sees and admires; she does not put on a face for the public – her famous smile and warmth are completely genuine. Although the Queen Mother turns her public engagements into a joy for herself and an unforgettable pleasure for those whom she meets, her motivation comes from service to the monarchy and, in her own words, 'to our Beloved Country'. As her friend Lord David Cecil has said, 'She has an innate sense of duty which was greatly enhanced by the King. And she is very patriotic.'

A favourite motto of the Queen Mother's is 'Your work is the rent you pay for the room you occupy on earth.' For eight decades, she has never once been in arrears with that rent and has been overpaying ever since she left the nursery. From the Civil List, the money voted each year by Parliament, in 1984 the Queen Mother received £334,400. Out of that sum she pays for her Household (her comptroller, secretaries, press officer and the like), her staff at Clarence House and their food, and all the operating expenses of running the highly efficient 'Royal Firm'. There can be few who disagree that the country does not receive its money's worth from the Queen Mother. Well into her eighties, she is still averaging 120 separate public engagements a year. She is loath to give up the patronage of a charity or institution (these still number over 300) and will do so only if she thinks that she cannot do it justice and that a replacement could contribute more. On the days that she has no outside engagements, she still works; she will be at her desk by 10 o'clock, writing letters and telephoning. She receives dozens of letters asking for help; although, of course, she cannot give financial support to all who write, she does see what can be done and will write to a possible source of help, passing on the name of the person concerned. For example, if the appellant is an ex-serviceman or widow she will notify their local branch of SSAFA (Soldiers', Sailors' & Airmen's Families Association), and will often check up on the result later on.

To date, the Queen Mother has made thirty-six overseas tours visiting forty different countries. Her list would make even the most experienced international traveller blanch – a list that includes three full tours of Australia and New Zealand and eight visits to Canada, two of which included a tour of the United States of America. These long, gruelling overseas trips, even with modern flights or the comfort of the Royal Yacht *Britannia*, are now too much for the Queen Mother, who today only makes short trips to Europe, but she is still much in demand at home. Her engagement book is as full as she can make it – if the Household think that an engagement would be too strenuous, the Queen Mother will reply, 'But that is my *favourite*,' and begs to have the invitation accepted. Wherever she goes her reputation precedes her; she has a great effect on those whom she meets. The crowds are always drawn out by her warmth and charm. An observer at what appeared to him as a humdrum engagement described the Queen Mother's appearance: 'She was in her best mood

The Queen Mother with officers and men of the Irish Guards in West Germany, after presenting them with the traditional shamrock on St Patrick's Day 1984

and spirits. She has that astonishing gift of being sincerely interested in dull people and dull occasions . . . she seemed really interested and spoke to almost all of them, putting them instantly at their ease. . . . Somehow she creates such an impression (indeed a radiance) of goodwill and good behaviour that no ill-feelings could live or breed in such an atmosphere.'

The Queen Mother never seems to tire of meeting new people – when asked what she liked best, she once wrote 'Making Friends' in a child's autograph book. She strongly believes that 'everyone is pleasant' and that if you find someone boring, then the fault lies with you for not being able to bring them out. Since childhood she has had that rare gift of being able to talk to anyone, whoever or wherever they are. To the Queen Mother, everyone is different and there is no set pattern in her conversation. At a visit to The Royal Hospital and Home for Incurables in south London, a patient said after her visit, 'She was really interested in us – not like some of the ladies who come and speak to you as a duty: we can tell.'

The Queen Mother has 'the common touch'. Although she is grand and regal, people can identify with her, they can feel 'at home' in her presence because she pitches the conversation at their level, where they will be most at ease. When she met the Beatles after a Royal Variety Performance, she asked where they were performing next. 'Slough,' John Lennon replied, to which the Queen Mother said, 'Oh, near us!' At an agricultural show, a small girl whispered to her, 'Ma'am, I've also met your daughter. Do you know she's the Queen?', to which the Queen Mother answered softly, 'Yes, isn't it exciting.' It is these witty and down-to-earth replies that are remembered. She will never refer to the Prince of Wales or to his brothers as Prince Charles, Andrew or Edward but simply as 'my grandson'.

Even in the largest crowds, the Queen Mother can make her presence felt. She has that knack of seeming to look into every single face and giving a special and personal smile to each person. She never forgets a face. She has always remembered the names and special details about any of the soldiers who convalesced at her childhood home of Glamis in Scotland during the First World War. It is a tremendous feat for there were 1,500 wounded who visited Glamis between 1914 and 1919. Her effect on even the most diehard re-

publicans is electric. As Duchess of York, it is said, she converted a committed Communist to an ardent royalist with just a glance during her first tour of New Zealand in 1927. Others have remarked, 'You feel you would go through hell for her.'

It was as Duchess of York that the Queen Mother began her long and devoted service to King and Country. It was entirely her outgoing personality and enthusiasm that softened the distant and formal side of the Royal Family. It was she, in her desire to meet people, who first disappeared into the crowds on what is now called a 'walkabout'. A policeman once lamented that he wished she were 'not quite so small' as he tried to protect her in an over-enthusiastic crowd. For all her stature and bearing, the Queen Mother is only 5 feet 2 inches tall, but if you meet her, you might well think her taller with her upright posture. Regardless of whoever else is in the room with her, you will notice only her. She is younger looking than her years, her bright, grey-blue eyes are shining and her complexion fair without excessive make-up. As she speaks, her hands move expressively and you are intrigued by the light, musical lilt of her bell-like voice. She is vibrant. As the late Poet Laureate, Sir John Betjeman, wrote for her eightieth birthday,

> . . . Waves of goodwill
> Go racing to meet you . . .

Above all, it is the Queen Mother's wonderful personality that shines out.

Those who know her well have so many of their own personal descriptions – 'instant sunshine'; 'the sort of person you would love to have as a neighbour'; 'an ageless person'; 'she's a real corker'. When the Queen Mother married King George V, on hearing that his daughter-in-law was occasionally unpunctual, was quick to remark, 'Ah, but if she weren't late, she would be perfect and how horrible that would be.' – a notion, no doubt, she would agree with. The Queen Mother's devoted Household enjoy working for her – everything is made 'such fun'. She has tea with them whenever possible and generally some of them lunch or dine with her. She has never been known to lose her temper in public and such is her calm presence no one can be ruffled – unless the Queen Mother herself is in some way threatened. She always finds her own special way of disarming a potentially dangerous situation. Once, when a crowd became too enthusiastic, she was heard to mutter, 'Please don't touch the exhibits!'

She gives, and expects and therefore receives, total loyalty from her Household and friends. She does not give her friendship lightly but once she has done so it is insoluble. She is forgiving of her Household and friends and can never believe ill of them for some breach of trust. But put to the test, the warrior-blood of her Scottish ancestors comes to the fore and she can be tough and even chilling when family or friends are threatened.

The Queen Mother is forceful in her likes and dislikes. Such is her popularity within her family and Household that she is denied nothing and that can be interpreted as extravagance. Lavish food, the best vintage wines, extensive building programmes and horses in training are expensive pastimes today and the Queen Mother indulges in them all.

She is famed for her ready wit and sense of fun. Whatever the occasion, if she is there 'it becomes a party'. She loves dancing and, after dinner, she will frequently organize an impromptu dance to gramophone records. A member of her family described her as having a 'great sense of humour – she can be very, very funny when she lets herself go'. Such a ready wit can also be very useful.

Never deterred by bad weather, the Queen Mother walks her corgis on the sands of Holkham, not far from Sandringham, the Queen's estate in Norfolk

During the tour of South Africa in 1947, when she was Queen, one of her Boer hosts said to her he could never forgive the English for having conquered his country, she replied, 'I do so understand. We feel much the same in Scotland.' Even in acute pain in hospital, she was able to joke about the medical bulletin, 'Of course the word comfortable has a different meaning for the surgeon than for the patient!' She can also make light of any disaster. On a tour of Tasmania in 1958, everything seemed to go wrong – the wind and rain soaked everybody, hats blew away, a fire-engine rattled through the Queen Mother's motorcade and the public address system failed. At the end of the tiring day, on reviewing the events she commented, 'I had a wonderful day and enjoyed everything!'

Apart from bronchial colds, the Queen Mother is an exceptionally fit person. She has great stamina, which comes from an active life both indoors and outside. She is at heart a country person – no weather is too bad to keep her from taking her corgis for a walk, often in driving rain, wearing her old mackintosh and felt hat. If suffering from a cold, she maintains that 'a strong wind will blow the germs away'. It will also take more than a strong wind, cold and rain to keep her off a National Hunt racecourse, although of late she has cut down on her attendances. However, she still takes *The Sporting Life* every day and watches the racing on television or on her video recorder. 'The Blower', the bookmakers' private racecourse

At the Royal Performance, at Her Majesty's Theatre, the Queen Mother receives Vivien Leigh with Laurence Olivier and Dame Sybil Thorndike in May 1954

commentary, has been installed at Clarence House so that she can keep up-to-date on the day's runners. Although not so active now as in former years, she is an expert and keen fisherwoman. Gardening, too, is another of her favourite pursuits – although she does not do any of the work, she is extremely knowledgeable about plants and has a great flair for planning and colour.

Many members of the Royal Family have been avid collectors and are knowledgeable in the Arts, but few have been as adventurous and as dedicated as the Queen Mother. She has collected modern pictures all her life, many by artists such as L. S. Lowry and often before they became fashionable and expensive. A few, such as Edward Seago, became close friends as well as being collected. Other friends she has met through her love of the Arts were the late Lord Britten of Aldeburgh (Benjamin Britten) and Sir Peter Pears, the founders of the famous Aldeburgh Festival. She is also just as much at home at the ballet at Covent Garden Opera House (another friend is the choreographer, Sir Frederick Ashton) as at a Royal Variety Performance at the London Palladium.

The Queen Mother has attended every Royal Variety Performance in aid of the Entertainment Artistes' Benevolent Fund since she became Queen in 1936. She is now a joint patron of the Fund with the Queen. At a special performance for the Queen Mother in 1961, the French actor and singer Maurice Chevalier topped the bill of her favourite artists. When he began to sing the popular song, 'You must have been a beautiful baby', the house cheered the obvious allusion to the Queen Mother. When he ended the last line with 'Cos Majesty, look at you now!', he brought the house down as he echoed the opinion of the world.

CHAPTER ONE

An Enchanted Childhood

The local people call the house 'The Bury', short for St Paul's Walden Bury, in the Hertfordshire village of St Paul's Walden near Hitchin. It is a Bowes-Lyon family house and successive generations have lived there since a Bowes forebear-by-marriage built it in the eighteenth century. It is an imposing house, of pretty, red brick set in sweeping grounds that were reputedly laid out by Le Nôtre, the French gardener of Versailles fame. The house is famous, not so much for its undeniable architectural merit nor its pleasant gardens, but as the early home of Queen Elizabeth the Queen Mother.

It is one of those splendid British anomalies that no one is absolutely certain where Queen Elizabeth the Queen Mother was born although she was an earl's youngest daughter, the daughter-in-law of a sovereign, a Royal Duchess, the Queen Consort and is mother of the Sovereign. Her father, then Lord Glamis, had somehow neglected to register her birth in the statutory time, within forty-two days. This he rectified later in Hitchin, the town near St Paul's Walden, thus giving rise to the supposition that she was born at 'The Bury'. It is, however, far more likely that she was born in their London house in St James's Square.

What is known for sure is that the Honourable Elizabeth Bowes-Lyon was born on 4 August 1900. At her baptism at the local parish church of All Saints on 23 September, she was christened Elizabeth Angela Marguerite – Elizabeth a family name of the Lyon family and Marguerite after the sister of the 1st Duke of Portland, a Cavendish-Bentinck ancestress of her mother. Elizabeth was

St Paul's Walden Bury, the Queen Mother's childhood home; it was designed in part by Robert Adam and is noted for its fine garden

The Earl and Countess of Strathmore and their family in the Drawing Room of Glamis Castle. A painting by Alexandro Calani Chili, 1909

the ninth child of Lord and Lady Glamis, with five brothers and two sisters, while a third sister, Violet Hyacinth, had died of diphtheria seven years earlier. Elizabeth was not the last child, however, for two years later the Bowes-Lyon family was completed with the birth of David. With such an age gap between the first and last child – at David's birth in 1902 the eldest, Mary, was approaching nineteen, with Patrick (the Master of Glamis), John, Alexander, Fergus, Rose and Michael, who was nearly nine, in between – it was inevitable that the two youngest, Elizabeth and David, should become especially close. Theirs was a deep bond that was to last throughout their lives. She referred to him as 'my darling Bruvver', while their mother referred to them both as 'my Benjamins' – an Old Testament analogy to Benjamin, the youngest and favourite of Jacob's many

sons. Like the youngest of any family, the Benjamins were spoiled, particularly Elizabeth, but to no ill effect.

When she was just a few weeks old, the daughter of a tenant farmer on the estate, Clara Cooper Knight, was engaged to look after the new baby. Affectionately known as 'Alla', she was to stay with the family for eleven years. Then, after a spell of fifteen years with Elizabeth's eldest sister, Mary, who married Lord Elphinstone, she was to return to care for Elizabeth's own children, the Princesses Elizabeth and Margaret. Elizabeth was a forward child, crawling and talking at a young age. Her mother wrote to a friend, 'Elizabeth is learning to walk – very dangerous.'

The Bowes-Lyon children, who thought themselves more a 'clan' than a family, were unusually fortunate in their parents. Although Elizabeth was born at the very end of Queen Victoria's reign, and brought up in the Edwardian era, Lord and Lady Glamis did not believe in the contemporary tradition that 'children should be seen and not heard'. Lady Glamis, of whom a friend once said, 'If there be a genius for family life, she has it,' took an active interest in the raising of her children herself. She was universally adored, particularly by her own family. In a later interview, one of her daughters remembered her as '. . . a very wonderful woman, very go-ahead and so upright. She had terrific sympathy. . . . She was extremely artistic. She sewed lovely embroidery, which she designed herself. She had an extremely good ear for music, she would go to a concert and listen to the music, and come back and play it perfectly.' Above all, she had the tremendous gift of being able to make friends and to set the nervous at total ease. Like Lady Glamis, her husband was a deeply religious man. Lord Glamis was essentially a country man and an above average sportsman. Quiet, with beautiful manners and a deep sense of duty, he cared greatly for his family and estates, as well as for his servants and tenantry.

Such talents were passed on to Elizabeth at a very early age. Even at the age of three, this engaging child with round cheeks and grey-blue eyes charmed her parents' guests. The many visitors to 'The Bury' remember being met by her at the door and, in the absence of a grown-up, being taken to their rooms – a slow process as she could barely manage the stairs. When she was a little older, they recalled the self-assured way she rang for tea and entertained them until her mother arrived. Such qualities were quickly recognized and used by the family whenever conversation dragged. 'Send for Elizabeth,' was a familiar cry, and the unselfconscious little girl would lead a difficult guest off with 'let us talk' – a conversation that could last anything up to three-quarters of an hour. Later Lord Gorell, the author, was to write,

To every lover of children she had about her that indefinable charm that bears elders into fairyland. In the simplest and most unconscious way she was all-conquering. In addition to the charm of especially winsome childhood, she had, even then, that blend of kindliness and dignity that is the peculiar characteristic of her family. She was small for her age, responsive as a harp, wistful and appealing one moment, bright-eyed and eager the next with a flashing smile of appreciative delight, an elphin creature swift of movement . . . swift of intelligence, alive with humour, able to join in any of the jokes, and [later] touchingly and sometimes amusingly loyal to her friends.

It is not difficult to see these same, and so many other, sterling qualities in the Queen Mother today as in the small child then.

When Elizabeth was just three and a half, her paternal grandfather died and her father succeeded as the 14th Earl of Strathmore. Elizabeth became the Lady Elizabeth Bowes-Lyon, which can have meant little to her, and, anyway, she was already known within the family as 'Princess' – a prophetic nickname. In addition to the estates at St Paul's Walden Bury, which he already owned, Lord Strathmore inherited what was originally a Bowes property, Streatlam Castle in Durham and the family seat, Glamis Castle, Tayside, on the east coast of Scotland.

It was said of the Strathmores that they were immensely grand, 'so grand that you didn't

An early photograph of Elizabeth Bowes-Lyon

notice that they were grand at all'. Like royalty, they travelled between their houses at set times each year with their servants. August and September was the time for the visit to Glamis and Elizabeth was there for her first birthday. Although born in England of an English mother, albeit with a drop of French blood, the Queen Mother considers herself truly Scots. Rightly so, for there could be no more romantic setting than Glamis Castle, nor more noble or ancient lineage than the Lyon family in Scotland.

The castle and family go hand in hand, as they have done for over six hundred years. At the succession of Robert II as King of Scotland in 1371, Sir John Lyon, known as 'The White Lyon' because of his fair colouring, was Keeper of the Privy Seal. As a reward for service to his Sovereign, Sir John was granted the lands of 'the thanage of Glamis', which, at that time, was just a royal hunting lodge. On his marriage to the king's daughter Jean, he was granted further lands of the 'thanedom of Tannadyce' as a dowry. From then on, the Lyon family have been inextricably linked with the monarchy and history. The White Lyon's grandson, Patrick, was sent as a hostage to England for James I of Scotland and on his release was created Lord Glamis. Three generations later, the wife of the 6th Lord Glamis, Lady Jean Douglas was burned alive as a witch in Edinburgh.

> With the great commiseration of the people, being in the prime of her years, of a singular beauty, and suffering all, though a woman, with manlike courage, all men conceiving that it was not this act [witchcraft] but the hatred which the king [James V] carried to her brothers.

James V subsequently stayed at the impoverished Glamis removing family treasures and, as the Exchequer Rolls show, 'twelve great silver flagons [which] were melted down to supply silver for the royal mint'. However, the fortunes of the Lyon family improved after that – the 9th Lord Glamis, responsible for much of the rebuilding of the castle, was captain of the King's guard and a privy councillor and as such created the 1st Earl of Kinghorne by James I of England and VI of Scotland. The title of Strathmore was added to the earldom by Charles II. Still loyal to the Stuart cause, the 5th Earl was killed at the Battle of Sheriffmuir in the Jacobite rebellion in 1715.

The Bowes family of Streatlam Castle and Gibside in Durham entered the Lyon family with the marriage of the heiress, Mary Bowes, to the 9th Earl of Strathmore in 1763. By Act of Parliament, the Strathmores adopted the name of Bowes, and the family became known as Bowes-Lyon.

The Castle of Glamis is one of the oldest continuously inhabited dwellings in Scotland. It has prospered and waned with the fortunes of the family, who have lived there since the original grant of the royal hunting lodge. Glamis is built of a rich, pink stone quarried from Hunter's Hill at the point where the Sidlaw Hills merge into the Strathmore valley – hence the family title. Built in the Scottish Baronial style, it is all that a Scottish castle should be – grand, imposing, romantic, not a little awesome and steeped in history. Although parts of the castle predate the mid-fifteenth-century wings, the real building began in the early 1600s with further nineteenth-century additions. The surrounding walls were pulled down (to the subsequent fury of Sir Walter Scott, a frequent visitor – his room, now called the Sir Walter Scott room, still has the original tartan hangings) to make way for the new grounds that were thought to have been laid out by Capability Brown in the 1770s. A more recent gardener at Glamis was Elizabeth's mother, Lady Strathmore, who, with great knowledge and artistic foresight, laid out the formal gardens surrounded by a yew hedge that can be seen today.

Glamis Castle really comes to life in its true magic as the setting for Shakespeare's play *Macbeth*. Whether he visited the castle, as he is reputed to have done before writing the play, or not, he has indeed caught the spirit of the place with these lines of the king in the First Act:

DUNCAN: This castle hath a pleasant seat; the air
    Nimbly and sweetly recommends itself
    Unto our gentle senses.

That mythical Thane of Glamis is no forebear of the Queen Mother, but the original guard room of the castle is still called Duncan's Hall.

With a background that is such an integral part of Scottish history, it is no wonder that when Elizabeth learned to read at a very early age, history was her favourite subject. Years later, when she first met Queen Mary, it was her knowledge of history, among her many other attributes, that so impressed her future mother-in-law.

Glamis is situated beside Dean Water, twelve miles north of Dundee. It has been the seat of the Lyon family since the fourteenth century

In recalling their childhood homes, David Bowes-Lyon, Elizabeth's 'darling Bruvver', regarded 'Glamis as a holiday place, Streatlam as a visit and St Paul's as "Home"'. Visits to Streatlam ceased when the estate was sold to pay off death duties a few years after her grandfather died and the castle was pulled down shortly afterwards. There was also a town house, 20 St James's Square, but in those early years, trips to London for Elizabeth were mostly confined to special treats like a visit to the pantomime at the Drury Lane Theatre after Christmas – or checkups with the dentist. A childhood friend who played with her in Hyde Park and who remembers her well is the historian Lord David Cecil. Years later, he recalled her 'sweetness and sense of fun; and

A private family photograph of Elizabeth – her girlish good looks were soon to show a regal serenity

a certain roguish quality. The personality I see now was there already.' There were also endless children's parties. At one such party given by the Countess of Leicester, Elizabeth enchanted a shy boy called Bertie by offering him the cherries off the top of her cake. Bertie was Prince Albert, second son of George V, and the future husband of that five-year-old little girl.

Shortly before her marriage, Elizabeth is recorded (strangely in the third person) by her friend Lady Cynthia Asquith, reminiscing over her enchanted childhood at 'The Bury':

At the bottom of the garden, where the sun always seems to be shining, is THE WOOD – the haunt of fairies, with its anemones and ponds, and moss-grown statues, and the BIG OAK under which she reads and where two ring doves, Caroline-Curley-Love and Rhoda-Wrigley-Worm, contentedly coo in their "Ideal Home".

There are carpets of primroses and anemones to sit on, and she generally has tea either in the

shadow of the statue of Diana or near another very favourite one called the 'Running Footman' or the 'Bounding Butler' (to grown-up people known as the Disc-Thrower). These statues live in cut-out grassy places, and sometimes there are wild strawberries around them, sometimes bee-orchises.

Very often she gets up wonderfully early – about six o'clock – to feed her chickens and make sure they are safe after the dangers of the night. The hens stubbornly insist on laying their eggs in a place called the FLEA HOUSE, and this is where she and her brother go and hide from Nurse.

Nothing is quite so good as the FLEA HOUSE, but the place called the HARNESS ROOM is very attractive too. Besides hens there are bantams whose eggs-for-tea are-so-good.

The Coronation edition of *The Times* in 1937 reprinted an article written by the Queen some years earlier on her childhood.

Here were all things that children could desire – dogs and tortoises, Persian kittens and 'Bobs' the Shetland pony, hay to make, chickens to feed, a garden, a friendly stillroom, the attic of a tumbledown brewhouse to play truant in, bullfinches to tame, fields to roam, flowers to love, ripe apples to drop, providently, about the head and on wet days the books that are best read on the floor in front of the fire . . .

As the Queen Mother remembered, life at 'The Bury' was magical and spent mostly out of doors in the company of her brother David. They knew every inch of the extensive grounds – especially the 'cloisters', which were wide, grassy rides cut through woods of oak and beech, silver birch and firs from the house. There was their garden, which they tended with love, giving their plants their own made-up names. There was the lake and a punt to fish from and a tiny island to explore. The centre of Elizabeth's fantasy world was the 'flea house', a loft over a disused granary with a rickety staircase – supposedly inaccessible to grown-ups, particularly nursery maids. There, she and her brother would keep a store of biscuits stolen from the kitchen, apples that 'conveniently' dropped in the orchard, sweets bought with precious pocket-money and even a packet of 'Woodies' (Woodbine cigarettes) and matches.

As in all country houses, animals played a great part in the life of the family. Besides the 'Persian kittens and tortoises', there were always

dozens of dogs – her father's and brothers' shooting dogs in the kennels (Lord Strathmore was an exceptional shot) as well as her mother's and sisters' assorted lap-dogs. There were horses in the stables, and a favourite of Elizabeth's was a Shetland pony named Bobs. The affection she had for

'The Benjamins' – Elizabeth aged four with her two-year-old brother, David

Portrait of Elizabeth aged six. She was remembered by family friends and staff as an enchanting child but also showing an occasional mischievous streak

Bobs was amply repaid, for the devoted pony would follow her around the garden like a dog, even climbing the steps onto the terrace and into the house. The housekeeper, Mrs Thompson, remembered Elizabeth teaching her pony to beg for lumps of sugar, the reward being offered at her window.

Birds, too, were favourite pets. Apart from her hens and bantams that she cared for herself, Elizabeth delighted in a tame bullfinch called Bobby that came into the day-nursery at meal times and, strutting up and down the table, would feed off the children's plates. But Bobby was caught by a cat. His remains were placed in David's pencil box lined with rose petals which was buried in their own garden to an impromptu funeral oration and rare tears from Elizabeth. Other dead birds were accorded similar honours.

An early lesson in the fairness of life was learned the hard way when a favourite pig, a black Berk-shire called Lucifer, was given to the church fête as a raffle prize. Elizabeth and her brother were horrified: they raided their money boxes and solicited loans from family and staff to buy up all the tickets. Unfortunately, they could only corner half the market – even-money on the pig's safe return. Lady Luck was not with them and the pig Lucifer was lost forever, to many tears. Tears, however, were uncommon with the 'Benjamins', although on one occasion David was given a mock thrashing with a hunting crop for some misdemeanour; while he dissolved into peals of laughter, Elizabeth sobbed.

For Elizabeth, the house itself was no less enchanting than the gardens. The Bowes-Lyon 'clan' were all brought up in the day and night nurseries in the west wing before graduating to their own rooms in the main house. The rooms were furnished in a style that was typical of the age – the day nursery being homely with heavy, well-worn furniture, a large brass fender round the fire and cupboards filled with much-loved toys, that were worn through years of use. There was a large Victorian screen with a collage of bright cut-outs and, on the wall, pictures torn out of magazines and framed by one of the gardeners. It was not all play for Lady Strathmore's 'Benjamins'. She told them stories, especially Bible stories, and taught them to read, later adding elementary music and drawing to the curriculum. Elizabeth and her brother went to the Sun Hotel in Hitchin for dancing lessons and there was plenty of opportunity to practise at home. There was 'a wonderful chest full of period costumes and the wigs that went with their gorgeousness' for dressing-up, for charades and to entertain parents and friends. The dressing-up box had a further use at Glamis. With her wonderful gift for story-telling, Elizabeth would regale unwary guests with stories of how the castle was haunted by 'Old Beardie', the ghost of Earl Beardie, and the 'Grey Lady', then dress up a dummy and leave it in a dimly lit corridor for a hapless guest to discover.

Such was the charm and general well-being of the Strathmore family, there was little need for enforced discipline. Once, for no apparent reason, the six-year-old Elizabeth took a pair of scissors to some sheets, but she owned up to her mother, who reproved her merely by saying 'Elizabeth' in

Lady Elizabeth Bowes-Lyon. A watercolour by Mabel E. Hankey, 1908

Mabel Dankey.

Elizabeth, aged nine, at Glamis where the Strathmores spent the summer holidays until the First World War

a sad voice. Apart from family and friends, Elizabeth was adored by all, or nearly all. She had a passion for chocolate cake, a craving that was indulged by the housekeeper, who remembered her tripping downstairs saying 'Mrs Thompson, have you any of those nice creams left for us?' and she would then help herself to her favourites. The cook was not so benevolent. 'The little imp,' she wrote. 'I was forever chasing her out of my kitchen.'

By the time their first governess, a Frenchwoman called Mlle Lang, had arrived, Elizabeth had already shown a lively and agile mind. Her new governess, whom she called 'Madé' (short for

Mademoiselle), remembered her at their first meeting as 'an enchanting child with tiny hands and feet and rose-petal colouring'. Elizabeth greeted her with, 'I do hope you will be happy here'. She was and she stayed for six years, teaching both Elizabeth and David.

The 'Benjamins' were inseparable, even when they went to a day school in Marylebone High Street in London when 'Madé' briefly returned to France. Elizabeth enjoyed the school and her lessons, although once she was reproved for precociously starting an essay on *The Sea* in Greek – *Thalassa, Thalassa* (the sea, the sea). At the end of two terms, she returned to the schoolroom with 'Madé' at 'The Bury'. Later, other governesses were engaged, some more appealing than others – once when Elizabeth was set an essay, all she wrote on the page was, 'Some governesses are nice, others are not.'

When David had to go away to school in 1912, Elizabeth missed her brother desperately. Once again, Lady Strathmore tried sending her to a London school so that she would meet girls of her own age. After two terms she left, having won the literature prize, and returned to the schoolroom at 'The Bury'. While in London, she also went to music and dancing lessons; these she continued after she left the day school, travelling up from 'The Bury' once a week. A great success, she was chosen to give the star performance at the end-of-term concert after only six months' tuition.

In 1913, a German temporary governess, Kathie Kuebler, was engaged for the Easter holidays. Her first impression of her new pupil was that 'she was charming to look at, a small, delicate figure with a sensitive, somewhat pale little face, dark hair and very beautiful, violet-blue eyes . . . a child far more mature and understanding than her age warranted'. Elizabeth responded to her, and Fraulein Kuebler's appointment was made permanent. They worked well together, Elizabeth perfecting her German and French while she continued with her other studies.

It was typical of Elizabeth to achieve everything at 'well below average age'. By Edwardian standards, she was exceptionally young when she graduated first from nursery, then to the schoolroom, and then to the dining-room to lunch with

Lady Elizabeth dressed up for a dancing lesson at Glamis, aged nine

her parents and their eminent friends that included elder statesmen such as Lord Rosebery and several former Viceroys of India. Elizabeth made a bright addition to the table.

Although she very much missed her brother while he was away at Broadstairs, his prep school in Kent, they could at least correspond and they were united during the holidays. In London they were allowed to go to the theatre on their own as often as their slender pocket-money would allow – their 'purses never bulged'. At Glamis for the summer holidays of 1913, the whole family was united again for what was to be the last time. Elizabeth's married sisters and brothers came with their spouses and children and a constant stream of visitors filled the twenty-eight guest bedrooms. There were endless games of tennis and tennis tournaments. Cricket matches were always popular and the Castle team, made up of Bowes-Lyons, their guests, tenants and servants, would take on local teams such as the Dundee Drapers, who once presented Lord Strathmore with a new Panama hat to mark his 'hat-trick' against them. As usual, Lord Strathmore, his sons and guests shot driven grouse on his moors, while Elizabeth followed for the picnic lunch on her aged donkey. However, she much preferred fishing. She fished the Dean, an adequate trout river that flowed through the garden or one of the streams or lochs on the estate. Throughout her life, the Queen Mother has remained a keen and competent fisherwoman.

It was during the summer of 1913 that Lady Strathmore finished laying out the formal gardens at Glamis, each with their yew or beech hedges. In the evening, after dinner, there were impromptu dances or charades and dressing-up. Lord Gorell, a guest at that time, later recalled those heady days,

> . . . brothers and sisters, all on the happiest terms together at Glamis – a great and historic house, no stiffness, no aloofness anywhere, no formality except the beautiful old custom of having the two pipers marching round the table at the close of dinner, followed by a momentary silence as the sound of their bagpipes dies away gradually in the distance of the castle. It was all so friendly and so kind, days of such whole-hearted delightful youth under the gracious guidance of Lady Strathmore, kindest and most understanding of hostesses, and the old castle re-echoed with fun and laughter. No wonder little Elizabeth came

up to me once as my visit was nearing its end and demanded: 'But why don't you *beg* to stay?'

The summer holidays over and back at 'The Bury', Elizabeth concentrated on taking her Junior Oxford Exams, which she passed 'with distinction' again well below the average age. Plans were made for her to travel in Europe the next summer with Fräulein Kuebler, but the rumblings of war with Germany soon put paid to these and her German governess returned to her homeland. War was finally declared on 4 August 1914, the day of Elizabeth's fourteenth birthday. The longstanding birthday treat, a visit to London's Coliseum theatre, was not cancelled as Elizabeth had feared, but the scene inside was one of wild enthusiasm and of patriotic fervour. That night, Elizabeth could hear the crowds as they marched down The Mall to Buckingham Palace to acclaim the King. Elizabeth had had an enchanted childhood with hardly a care in the world, but the First World War was to change all that, as it did for everyone. Nothing would be the same any more.

Lady Elizabeth celebrated her fourteenth birthday on the day the First World War broke out. The war was to last for most of her teens

CHAPTER TWO

Growing up

The war that people said would be over by Christmas lasted for another four terrible years. For the first time, Elizabeth spent Christmas at Glamis, but it was very different from the usual happy family party. On that Christmas night, Elizabeth stood in the Castle crypt in a circle of newly arrived soldiers around a tall Christmas tree, the light from a hundred candles reflecting off the suits of armour against bare stone walls. In the dining-room, there were lines of neat, white beds that were always to be occupied, until the Christmas of 1919, for the castle had been converted into a convalescent home for wounded soldiers.

For the Bowes-Lyon family, those early days of the First World War were full of excitement and action. Elizabeth's four brothers joined up immediately – Patrick, John and Fergus enlisted in The Black Watch (the local regiment to Glamis) and Michael went into the Royal Scots. Her older, unmarried sister, Rose, trained as a nurse in a London hospital. Besides the hectic preparations of the Bowes-Lyon family, there was the excitement of two weddings when both Fergus and John married shortly before their battalions were posted overseas.

Later on, the Queen Mother was to recall those early days of the First World War as 'the bustle of hurried visits to chemists for outfits of every sort of medicine, and to gunsmiths to buy all the things that people thought they wanted for a war, and found they didn't'. At Glamis, the preparations continued. 'Lessons were neglected, for we were so busy knitting, and making shirts for the local battalion – the 5th Black Watch. My chief occupa-

Ever since she could remember, dogs have been a much loved and important part of the Queen Mother's life

Glamis became a convalescent home for wounded soldiers. Lady Elizabeth, with her sister, Lady Rose, a nurse, welcomes one of the wounded in 1915

tion was crumpling-up tissue paper until it was so soft that it no longer crackled, to put into the lining of sleeping bags.'

When Rose finished her nursing training, she took charge at Glamis. Elizabeth was considered too young and unqualified to do any nursing, but her contribution to the well-being of the wounded was higher than any medical skill. Elizabeth, with her mother, welcomed each soldier wearing the blue flannel uniform of the wounded at the front door. It can only have been daunting for these soldiers when they entered a grand castle as the guests of the nobility, but Elizabeth, with her charm and sweet nature, quickly set them at their ease. She would see that they had everything they needed. She bought them little presents, cigarettes and tobacco from the village shop and wrote letters home for them, enclosing their photograph, which she took herself. She would play the piano and join in their singsongs, even playing whist during the long winter evenings. Not surprisingly, Elizabeth was adored by them all, she 'teased and charmed them into good

spirits . . . and helped to restore them to normality. Some of the men were shattered in body and spirit. She then had her early lessons in complete, selfless control, in the iron discipline and sense of duty that lie under a smile.'

One patient, Corporal Ernest Pearne, remembered his time at Glamis as 'the happiest period of my life; every comfort, every care, an abundance of excellent food and nothing to do but be happy and get fat' – a far cry from the horrors of the trenches and the Flanders mud. He recalled the first time he met Elizabeth, 'she had the loveliest pair of blue eyes I'd ever seen – very expressive, eloquent eyes that could speak for themselves. She had a very taking habit of knitting her forehead just a little now and then when speaking and her smile was a refreshment. I noticed in particular a sort of fringe at the front of her shapely head. Her teeth were even and very white and well set, and when speaking she struck me as being the most charming little lady and a most delightful companion.' It was just that delightful companionship that all the soldiers grew to love.

They loved her for her humour. Once, when David came back from school, Elizabeth dressed him up as an elderly female cousin in a long skirt, cloak, veil, furs and a 'becoming hat' and took him round the ward. He played the part beautifully, talking to each soldier as if a distinguished visitor and only the next day was the ruse rumbled. The resulting comments from the patients were far from suitable for the ears of a 'maiden aunt'.

Just as life at Glamis and 'the Countess of Strathmore's Hospital' was settling down to a steady routine, tragedy struck the family. Fergus returned to Glamis for a short leave in 1915 to see his two-month-old daughter, Lusia. Three days after he rejoined his regiment he was killed at the Battle of Loos. He was just twenty-six years old. His death was a terrible shock, particularly to his mother. The soldiers, all inevitably close to the family, felt his death deeply and signed a letter of sympathy to Lady Strathmore. They agreed not to use the billiard table or play games on the lawn and even used a side entrance so as not to disturb the family in their grief. It was typical of Lady Strathmore to send word down that they should carry on exactly as before. Her grief affected her health and now more of the burden of running her home and the responsibility of the hospital passed to Elizabeth. When Rose left home to marry a young Royal Navy Commander, William Leverson Gower (pronounced Lucen Gore), the responsibility that fell on Elizabeth, still only sixteen, was even greater. She coped in a manner far beyond her years and it was that fearful experience, earned at first hand, that was to stand her in such good stead in the Second World War.

One day at the end of 1916, Elizabeth displayed her courage and calm in a crisis: she noticed sparks and smoke billowing out of one of the upper rooms in the central keep of the castle. Her forethought saved Glamis, for she not only telephoned the local fire brigades at Glamis and Forfar, but Dundee as well. When the local fire brigades arrived, their hoses were too short to reach the River Dean, a few hundred yards away. By the time the Dundee Fire Brigade arrived, the heat had melted a lead tank in the roof and thousands of gallons of water flooded down the staircase. Without a moment's thought, Elizabeth and her brother David and a few of the estate staff,

armed with brooms, positioned themselves outside the principal rooms and swept the water on down to the stone corridors and halls. That crisis past, Elizabeth then organized a human chain to pass out as many pictures and as much furniture as they could manage. Although Glamis was badly damaged, the majority of its treasures was saved, but it was many years before it was completely restored to its former glory. But for Elizabeth and her calmness in a crisis, Glamis would have been lost. At the time the patients were at the local cinema. No one was injured except for the pride of one onlooker, who, on asking ridiculous questions of Elizabeth, received a curt – 'I've no time to make conversation!', to which he muttered, 'Who's yon prood lassie?'

After the death of Fergus, the family lived in daily dread of another telegram announcing the death of one of the other three brothers. Early in 1917, it was reported that Michael had been badly wounded in the head. He was presumed

Lady Strathmore, with Elizabeth and David, watched as fire swept through the tower at Glamis Castle in 1916

In 1917 Michael Bowes-Lyon was reported missing; fortunately he had only been taken prisoner

EARL'S SON MISSING.

The Hon. Michael Bowes-Lyon
Royal Scots.

dead at first but had been taken prisoner. Later, he had the chance of returning home in a prisoner exchange, but gave up his place for a brother officer.

The war dragged on for nearly two more years before Germany finally surrendered on 11 November 1918. The wounded were still sent to convalesce at Glamis for another year, the last one leaving just before Christmas 1919. In addition to the wounded, Australian and New Zealand officers stayed with the Bowes-Lyons as they waited for a ship home. In all, more than 1,500 wounded stayed at Glamis. They were all made to feel at home. They signed the visitors' book as they left, each one with some small present and a happy memory of the place and, above all, of the Lady Elizabeth Bowes-Lyon. In return, Elizabeth remembered them all, and in later years during her visits to all parts of Britain and the Commonwealth, she would renew old friendships with those who had convalesced at Glamis. One man echoed all the others when he said, 'She always made you feel you were the one person in the

Lord and Lady Strathmore and Elizabeth with some of the 1,500 Great War convalescents at Glamis

world she wanted to be seeing. It was great medicine!'

After the horrors and depredations of the First World War, London society ran fast and loose. It was the age of 'bobbed hair, short skirts and the long weekend'. After all Lady Elizabeth Bowes-Lyon had been through during those war years and, with her breeding, assured manner, charm and beauty, it would have been natural for her to gravitate to that gay set, but those who really knew her would have been very surprised if she had. Lord and Lady Strathmore were indeed old-fashioned, clinging to a life-style, values and manners of the pre-war era. Lady Elizabeth was very much their youngest unmarried daughter and, in her own way, old-fashioned. Lady Airlie, a Glamis neighbour, noted, she 'was very unlike the cocktail-drinking, chain-smoking girls who came to be regarded as typical of the 1920s'.

As befitted Lady Elizabeth's background, her parents gave her a 'coming-out' dance. She had a high temperature that day, but so as not to disappoint her friends, she went ahead with the dance. She enjoyed her dance and the rest of the 'Season'. A friend of her mother's wrote, 'Elizabeth Lyon is now out, and Cecilia [Lady Strathmore]

has had a dance for her. How many hearts will Elizabeth break?' The answer was more than a few.

She went to dances, to dinner parties, to the theatre and away for weekends, a popular guest wherever she went. She was unique in London society – one admirer described her as 'very kind and compassionate . . . and she could be very funny – which was rare in those circles. She was a wag.' She was noticed at Royal Ascot in a 'white lace frock with a hat with a distinct tendency to become a poke bonnet'. She soon established a reputation of being the 'best dancer in London' and was greatly sought after as a partner. She was also much in demand as a bridesmaid. In April 1920 she was chief bridesmaid to her great friend Lady Lavinia Spencer, a great-aunt of the present Princess of Wales, when she married Lord Annaly.

There were also trips abroad, one to Paris with her friend Diamond Hardinge, to attend a ball at the British Embassy, where Diamond's father, Lord Hardinge, was British Ambassador. One guest wrote of the scene:

> At last night's ball the rooms were perfect, and there were lots of pretty people in lovely gowns. The most charming sight there was Lady Elizabeth [Bowes-] Lyon, a bewitching little figure in rose colour, which set off her lovely eyes and dark eyebrows to perfection. She seemed to me the incarnation of fresh, happy, English girlhood: so bright, so natural with an absolutely enchanting smile and a look of incredible goodness and sweetness, shot with a delicious gleam of humour and fun, laughter and music, and yet with a sense of deep, eternal realities of life as foundations to it all. That would account for the thoughtful look on the brow, the quiet inner radiance that her face wears in repose, though superficially it would appear all sparkle and girlish fun. Certainly last night she stood out as an English rose, sweet, fresh as if the dew were still on it.

However much Lady Elizabeth loved the attractions of London, she was at heart a country girl. Her family and homes, both at 'The Bury' and Glamis, were still a focal point of her life and she had no wish to change this. She was an integral part of the estates and the community just as the welfare of the servants and tenantry were close to her, especially at Glamis. One particular post that she held was, indirectly, to affect her life

Lady Elizabeth had charm and beauty and remained a home-loving girl – photographed with her father.

dramatically and that was as District Commissioner of the Glamis and Eassie Parish Girl Guides. She was an able and popular Commissioner and later the Secretary of the London Headquarters was to write of her, 'Although she was only twenty-one at the time of her appointment as District Commissioner, Lady Elizabeth has been responsible for the whole of the training, recruiting and discipline of the Glamis branch for the past two years. She is an excellent officer, and has taken the keenest interest in her work.'

It was as Commissioner that Lady Elizabeth first met Princess Mary, the President of the Girl Guides, when she came to inspect the Glamis Guides. Princess Mary, later to be accorded the title of Princess Royal, was the only daughter of George V and Queen Mary. A firm and lasting friendship grew out of that meeting, and it was not

Prince Albert, Duke of York, aged twenty-three, second son of King George V and Queen Mary, 1918

Lady Elizabeth Bowes-Lyon became friends with Princess Mary, daughter of George V

long before Lady Elizabeth was part of the 'junior' Buckingham Palace set. Although the dance given by Lord and Lady Farquhar at their house in Grosvenor Square on 20 May 1920 is thought to be the occasion where Prince Albert, George V's and Queen Mary's second son, met Lady Elizabeth, it is more likely that they met at Buckingham Palace. Princess Mary gave impromptu gramophone *thé dansants* in her private apartments to which Lady Elizabeth soon became a frequent visitor. Prince Albert, or 'Bertie' to the family, was assigned to the Air Ministry in nearby Whitehall at that time and it is inconceivable that the two were not dancing partners at one or other of these gatherings.

Prince Albert had had the misfortune to be born on 14 December 1895 – the anniversary of not only the death of Queen Victoria's 'beloved husband', Prince Albert, but also of the death of their second daughter, Princess Alice. However, the Queen was philosophical and wrote, 'I have a feeling that it may be a blessing, for the dear little boy may be looked upon as a gift from God.' Throughout his early life, he remained under the shadow of his older brother, the Prince of Wales, known within the family as David, and, to a lesser extent, his father's favourite, Princess Mary. His parents were loving in their way, but they could not express their feelings to their children, who grew up much in awe of them. He developed a dreadful stammer, thought to be the result of being forced to write with his right hand when he was naturally left-handed. Prince Albert's time at Osborne and the Royal Naval College, Dartmouth, was undistinguished, but he was mentioned in dispatches – as a midshipman under the pseudonym Mr Johnson, he was in command of a gun turret aboard HMS *Collingwood* at the Battle of Jutland in 1916. To his disappointment, he was invalided out of the Royal Navy, but he transferred to a branch of the future Royal Air Force. From there, he went up to Cambridge

An early scene from Prince Albert's childhood. Queen Victoria with some of her family at Osborne House circa 1899. The Duke of York (left) holds Bertie while David, in the white sailor suit, and Mary sit with their mother, the Duchess

Below left *Prince Albert (later Duke of York and George VI), aged six, and* below right *he stands between his elder brother Prince Edward (later Edward VIII and Duke of Windsor) and his sister Princess Mary (later the Princess Royal)*

University, where he read economics, history and civics and, later, devoted his considerable talents and energy to industrial relations and the setting up of camps for boys from all walks of life. Despite having carved himself a particular niche in life, difficult even today in Royal circles, he was still painfully shy and somewhat serious with a fierce temper. His qualities, often hidden by self-effacement, were his humanity, warmth, high principles and a deep religious faith.

However, the Farquhars' dance in 1920 was the turning-point of his life. Lady Airlie wrote, 'He [Prince Albert] told me long afterwards that he had fallen in love that evening, although he did not realize it until later.' His father, recognizing at last his son's qualities, created him Duke of York that summer. He excelled in other areas, too, and won the RAF doubles championships at Wimbledon with his friend and equerry Wing Commander Louis Greig. He also engineered meetings with Lady Elizabeth. A friend of all the Bowes-Lyon brothers, he was often invited to join in their

The Duke of York, seated behind Lady Elizabeth on the left, was a frequent shooting and tennis guest at Glamis and St Paul's Walden Bury

entertainments. Lady Elizabeth liked him well enough, but marriage, to anyone, was out of the question for the time being. She was greatly enjoying her full life. Apart from the social aspect, she was also busy looking for a new London house for her parents as the lease of 20 St James's Square had come to an end. She settled on 17 Bruton Street, near Berkeley Square, a house that was to become famous as the birthplace of a future queen.

Once again, the ill-health of her mother left Lady Elizabeth with more than her share of responsibility in coping with the running of Glamis and the large and constant house parties. It was a task that she rose to willingly, and executed with her usual brand of cheerfulness and calm. Among the guests was the Duke of York, who was asked to stay for the opening of the grouse season on 12 August. He wrote to his mother, 'It is delightful here. Elizabeth is very kind to me. The more I see her, the more I like her' – something of an understatement. When Queen Mary was staying with her friend and Lady-in-Waiting Lady Airlie, at nearby Cortachy Castle, she went over to Glamis, ostensibly to see the castle but in reality to meet Lady Elizabeth. She was much impressed with her young hostess, although

David Bowes-Lyon's (centre back) private family photograph of Queen Mary's visit to Glamis, 1920. With the Queen are her friends Lady Airlie and Lady Strathmore who sits beside Princess Mary. Lady Elizabeth, known as 'Buffy' (middle row, centre) stands between her father and friends

observers jumped to the conclusion that she had her wayward eldest son, the Prince of Wales, in mind when she made the trip. She confided in Lady Airlie, 'She [Lady Elizabeth] seems a charming girl, but I don't know her very well.'

Not long afterwards, in the spring of 1921, the Duke of York plucked up enough courage to propose to Lady Elizabeth. He first informed his parents of his intention, to which his father, although pleased with his choice, typically replied, 'You will be a lucky fellow if she accepts you.' His proposal was gently turned down and, in retrospect, it is not difficult to see why. Again, it is Lady Airlie, in her autobiography *Thatched with Gold*,

who provides the answer. 'She was frankly doubtful and afraid of the public life which would lie ahead of her as the King's daughter-in-law.' It can only have been a daunting proposition for a girl not yet twenty-one to take on such a position. Once locked into the system, there would be no way out and the Court of George V was even more restrictive than the Court of today. Princess Alice, Queen Victoria's granddaughter, who died in 1981, knew what it was like from first-hand experience and wrote, 'None but those trained from youth to such an ordeal can sustain it with amiability and composure.' But the experience of the war years at Glamis was superior to any Royal 'castle-bound' existence for her role as future Queen Consort. Lady Elizabeth also feared for her privacy and her beloved family life, which, naturally, she prized highly.

It was a bitter blow for the Duke of York. Lady Strathmore noted his sad face and added, 'I do hope he will find a nice wife who will make him happy. I like him so much and he is a man who will be made or marred by his wife.' Queen Mary was disappointed, too, as she believed that Lady Elizabeth was the 'one girl who could make Bertie happy'. Undeterred by his refusal, the Duke of York continued to live in hope of marrying Lady Elizabeth and tried to see her as often as possible. He stayed again at Glamis and was a frequent guest at 'The Bury' during the shooting season.

Lady Elizabeth had her first real taste of Royal pageantry when her friend Princess Mary asked her to be one of her bridesmaids when she married Viscount Lascelles [later the 6th Earl of Harewood] in February 1922. She looked wonderful in her

Lady Elizabeth Bowes-Lyon was one of eight bridesmaids at Princess Mary's marriage with Viscount Lascelles on 28 February 1922

bridesmaid's dress of 'cloth of silver with a silver rose at the hip on a lover's knot of blue' and a circlet of silver rose leaves on her head. She enjoyed it all enormously and sat next to the Duke of York at the wedding breakfast.

Throughout 1922 Lady Elizabeth continued her life very much as before. The Duke of York continued to see her whenever possible, aided by such hostesses as Lady Airlie and Mrs Ronald Greville. The more he was with her and her family, the more he relaxed and his self-confidence grew. He revelled in the carefree informality and eternal sense of fun of the Bowes-Lyons, so different from his own family. As his official biographer, Sir John Wheeler Bennett, wrote, 'The happy badinage and affection of a large and closely knit family were a revelation, providing a climate of ideas to which he instantly responded and in which his own personality throve and blossomed. He was deeply in love.'

During that winter and the family Christmas spent at 'The Bury', Lady Strathmore noticed a distinct change in her daughter. Later she was to write, 'That winter was the first time I have ever known Elizabeth really worried. I think she was torn between her longing to make Bertie happy and her reluctance to take on the big responsibilities which this marriage must bring.' For the first time the positions were reversed – the Duke of York quietly confident and strengthened in his ties and affection for the Bowes-Lyon family, Lady Elizabeth unsure. Unlike his glamorous elder brother, the Prince of Wales, the Duke was a 'doer', not a talker – while David told the Welsh miners, 'Something must be done, something will be done,' Bertie went out and actually *did* something. He was determined that he was going to marry Lady Elizabeth, and early in the New Year he went to stay at 'The Bury' again.

On 13 January 1923, while the rest of the house party was at church, the Duke of York took Lady Elizabeth for a walk. There, in the woods and gardens that she had loved since childhood, he proposed to her again. This time she accepted and later the Duke sent a telegram to his parents who were at Sandringham. It read, 'ALL RIGHT – BERTIE' – the pre-arranged code that 'he had won her over at last'.

The Duke of York and Lady Elizabeth Bowes-Lyon – the official engagement photograph, January 1923

CHAPTER THREE

Duchess of York

Walter Bagehot wrote in *The English Constitution*, 'A Royal Family sweetens politics by the seasonable additions of pretty events. A princely marriage is the brilliant edition of a universal fact, and as such it rivets mankind.' Bagehot could have been writing of the events in 1923 rather than of fifty years earlier.

A Royal wedding was the tonic the country needed and it came at the right time. The euphoria of the victory celebrations was long over and the 'better world' that was promised was a long time in coming. One in six was unemployed and the 'Homes fit for Heroes' did not materialize. There was also growing unrest in Europe, troubles in Ireland and in India and the example of the Bolsheviks in Russia; Great Britain could have had its own serious civil disturbances. Yet, however divided the factions were in the country, they were at least united in their staunch loyalty to

their King, George V. When the King's son married a commoner – albeit the daughter of an earl – it was news to be greeted in every quarter.

The Court Circular carried the announcement on 16 January 1923:

> It is with the greatest pleasure that the King and Queen announce the betrothal of their beloved son the Duke of York to the Lady Elizabeth Bowes-Lyon, daughter of the Earl and Countess Strathmore, to which union the King has gladly given his consent.

The announcement of the engagement took the press by surprise. The scramble to gather facts

Above *The Duke of York and Lady Elizabeth*
Opposite *A study of Lady Elizabeth published in the Wedding Edition of the* Illustrated London News *on 28 April 1923*

about Lady Diana Spencer after her engagement to the present Prince of Wales was merely a 're-run' of the engagement of Lady Elizabeth Bowes-Lyon. Photographers 'doorstepped' at the Strathmores' new house in Bruton Street, hoping for a photograph or a comment. Lady Elizabeth did give one interview to *The Star*, but the King quickly put paid to any more. The Monarchy was prepared to bend slightly, but not that much.

The daily press was surprised by the announcement and the evening papers the day before had had her engaged to the Prince of Wales. Chips Channon, the ardent chronicler who had the art of being in the right place at the right time, wrote:

> I was so startled that I almost fell out of bed when I read the Court Circular. . . . We have all hoped, waited so long for this romance to prosper that we had begun to despair that she would ever accept him. . . . He is the luckiest of men and there's not a man in England today that doesn't envy him. The clubs are in gloom.

The next 'ordeal' for Lady Elizabeth was to go to Norfolk with her parents to discuss the wedding plans. Queen Alexandra still lived at Sandringham House, while the King and Queen Mary stayed in considerable discomfort in York Cottage, a rambling and ill-furnished warren. The King and Lady Elizabeth were instantly on the very best terms and the close bond of mutual respect and affection lasted for the rest of his life. She found him 'angelic' and wrote after his death:

> I miss him dreadfully. Unlike his own children I was never afraid of him, and in all the twelve years of having me as a daughter-in-law he never spoke one unkind or abrupt word to me, and was always ready to listen and give advice on one's silly little affairs. He was so kind and dependable. And when he was in the mood, he could be deliciously funny too!

Queen Mary, too, was enraptured by her future daughter-in-law. 'Elizabeth', she wrote in her diary, 'is so charming, so pretty and engaging and natural,' adding in a later entry, '. . . . a great addition to the family.' As the State Visit to Italy by the King and Queen in May could not be cancelled and there was no reason to delay the

The engaged couple en route *to Sandringham to discuss the wedding plans with the King and Queen*

One of a series of photographs taken at the time of Lady Elizabeth's engagement to the Duke of York

Lady Elizabeth Bowes-Lyon, by John St Helier Lander

Prince Albert, Duke of York, by John St Helier Lander

wedding, the date chosen was 26 April. The consent from the Privy Council was a formality – under the terms of the 1772 Royal Marriages Act, no British Royal descendant of George II can marry without the monarch's consent. A Royal precedent was also revived, as no Royal prince had married a commoner since the Duke of York (later James II) married Lady Anne Hyde, daughter of the Earl of Clarendon, secretly in 1660.

Back in London, Lady Elizabeth and the Royal Household were busy with the plans for her wedding, which was to take place in Westminster Abbey. Sackfuls of mail and telegrams arrived, all of which were answered by her personally. The BBC, still in its very early days, was denied permission to broadcast the wedding service for what seems today the most obtuse reason – it was thought in Royal circles that 'disrespectful people might hear it while sitting in public houses with their hats on' – a very far cry from the last Royal Wedding, when a television audience of 750 million people around the world watched the Prince and

Princess of Wales's marriage at St Paul's Cathedral in 1981 with the video cassette version breaking all sales records.

In the short time before the wedding there was much to do. Wedding presents flooded in from all quarters – at least £25,000 worth of gifts (in 1984 worth £347,000) had to be returned as the donors were not friends or in some way connected with the couple. Apart from his allowance from the Civil List of £26,000 a year, the Duke of York had no other income and few possessions. They asked for, and received, not only many useful and quite ordinary household items, such as linen sheets and blankets, but also grander presents such as the dinner service from the City of Worcester, silver from the City of London and a clock that played martial music from the City of Glasgow. More unusual presents included an oak chest filled with two dozen Wellington boots, galoshes and other rubber shoes from the Pattenmakers Guild and a thousand gold-eyed needles from the Livery Company of Needlemakers.

Above Lady Elizabeth leaving her home, 17 Bruton Street, for her wedding (right) at Westminster Abbey. Attended by eight bridesmaids, she wore a dress of ivory chiffon moiré and a lace train lent by Queen Mary

It was, of course, the family presents that meant the most to the couple. Lady Elizabeth gave her fiancé a platinum and pearl watch chain. Besides the engagement ring of a sapphire flanked by two diamonds, he gave her a diamond and pearl necklace with a matching pendant. The King gave her a writing table as well as turquoise and diamond jewellery and the Queen a necklet, brooches, ring and pendant of sapphires and diamonds. The Strathmores gave their daughter a platinum and diamond tiara and two pearl necklaces, one with a matching bracelet, and to their future son-in-law, a miniature of Lady Elizabeth by Mabel Hankey in a diamond-studded frame with the cypher 'E' under an earl's coronet on the top (see page 95).

A gloomy description survives from Mr Asquith, the former Prime Minister, who was asked to view the wedding presents,

I went in my knee breeches and medals after dinner where the rooms, big as they are, were very nearly crowded. There were huge glass cases like you see in the Bond St shops, filled with jewels and every kind of gilt and silver-ware: not a thing did I see that I would have cared to have or give. The poor little bride, everyone says is full of charm, stood in a row with the King and Queen and the bridegroom and was completely overshadowed.

That occasion can only have been unique for no one has overshadowed her since.

The name of the wedding dressmaker was kept a secret and details were released only shortly before the day. The dress was described in the *Vogue* Royal Wedding Number:

Lady Elizabeth's wedding gown is of ivory chiffon moiré, its slim straight lines suggesting a medieval Italian gown. Across the bodice are

Their Royal Highnesses, the Duke and Duchess of York, on their wedding day, 26 April 1923

bands of silver lamé ornamented with embroidery of seed pearls. A band of silver and pearls falls to the hem of the gown. From the waist falls a train of moiré and from the shoulders floats a mist of tulle edged with ivory Nottingham lace. A length of rare old lace, lent by Her Majesty the Queen, borders the veil, which is held by a chaplet of leaves. Gown from Handley-Seymour.

The dress was seen before the wedding in an exhibition staged by the Duchess of Portland to draw attention to the plight of the Nottingham lace workers. The trousseau was also revealed and consisted of fashionable clothes of the day, including one green flannel coat 'covered with Egyptian motifs of black and silver' – the Egyptian theme being popular after the opening of Tutankhamun's tomb by Lord Caernarvon and Howard Carter in 1922.

Lady Elizabeth's wedding day dawned wet and overcast although it cleared slightly as she left Bruton Street. She travelled with her father in a closed landau with an escort of four mounted policemen – still a commoner she was not entitled to a Sovereign's Escort from the Household Cavalry. On the way to Westminster Abbey, she drove through cheering crowds that numbered nearly a million. The King was to record in his diary, 'the sun actually came out as the bride entered the Abbey'. There she was joined by her eight bridesmaids. Her choice was needfully tactful – two of Queen Mary's nieces, Lady May Cambridge and Lady Mary Cambridge (the present Dowager Duchess of Beaufort), her two closest friends, Diamond Hardinge and Elizabeth Cator (who later married Michael Bowes-Lyon), two other friends, Lady Mary Thynne and Lady Katherine Hamilton, and two nieces, Elizabeth Elphinstone and Cecilia Bowes-Lyon. There was a slight pause as an equerry dashed to retrieve her handbag from her carriage and a cleric who had fainted was carried away. On the arm of her serious-faced father she processed up the aisle and, in an impulsive move, Lady Elizabeth placed her

Above left Huge crowds packed the streets to witness the procession from Westminster Abbey back to Buckingham Palace for the wedding breakfast Above right The wedding cake and below The bride and groom with their grim-faced parents

bouquet of white Yorkist roses and white heather on the tomb of the Unknown Warrior instead of at the Cenotaph in Whitehall, as Princess Mary had done after her wedding. She then joined the bridegroom at the altar steps.

The Duke of York wore the uniform of a Group Captain of the Royal Air Force with the Ribbon and Stars of the Orders of the Garter and the Thistle, the latter recently awarded to him by his father as a tribute to his Scottish bride. Two of his brothers, the Prince of Wales, in the uniform of the Grenadier Guards, and Prince Henry, in the uniform of the 10th Hussars, were his supporters (Royal parlance for best man). It was unfortunate that even on his wedding day, wearing the rather drab grey-blue of the Royal Air Force, the Duke of York should have been outshone by his popular and dashing elder brother.

The marriage service itself was performed by the Archbishop of Canterbury. The wedding ring was fashioned from a nugget of gold found in Wales, which was also large enough to make rings for the Queen, Princess Margaret, Princess Anne and, finally, the Princess of Wales. A life-long friend of the King's, Dr Cosmo Gordon Lang, Archbishop of York, gave the address, which included a special message for the new Duchess of York.

> You, dear bride, from your Scottish home have grown up from childhood among country folk and friendship with them has been your native air. So have you both been fitted to your place in the people's life, and your separate lives are now, till death, made one. You can not resolve that your wedded life will be happy, but you can and will resolve that it shall be noble. . . . The warm and generous heart of this people takes you today into itself. Will you not in response take that heart, with all its joys and sorrows, into your own? . . . On behalf of a nation happy in your joy, we bid you Godspeed.

The sun was shining when the bride and bridegroom left Westminster Abbey. The crowds cheered them all the way as they were driven in the open State Landau back to Buckingham Palace for the traditional balcony appearances and the austere wedding photographs. The wedding breakfast, in reality a lunch, was a huge affair with eight courses, ending in the cutting of the nine-foot-high cake. There were, mercifully, no speeches,

A happy Duke and Duchess of York depart for their honeymoon. The Duchess wore a grey crêpe dress

save a toast from the King to the bride and bridegroom, which in Royal circles is drunk in silence with no reply. At last, it was time to leave for their honeymoon and the Duke and Duchess of York travelled to Waterloo Station in an open carriage drawn by four grey horses. The crowd could only just glimpse her going-away dress, described the next day as:

a soft shade of dove-grey crêpe romain, which has a slightly beige tint in it, and is embroidered all in its own colour. The bodice has short sleeves, and there is a coatee made in a short band at the back. A travelling coat wrap in the same shape in crêpe morocain which has wheels of drawn thread work of its own material trimming it. Her going-away hat is a small affair in tones of brown with upturned brim and a feather mount at the side. She made this choice so that those in the crowd may not have their view impeded by a brim. With this dress are worn shoes of beige antelope in a sandal shape.

A train was waiting to take them on the first stage of their honeymoon to Bookham in Surrey, the local station for Polesden Lacey. The nineteenth-century house had been lent to them by Mrs Ronald Greville, who had entertained them both during their courtship. That night there was a family dinner party at 17 Bruton Street, where the Bowes-Lyon family had all agreed that the youngest daughter had not so much made a great match but 'basically something far more important. As one of the family put it, "Thank God she has married a good man." '

The honeymoon spent at Polesden Lacey was quiet. The Duke and Duchess of York walked in the extensive gardens and over the estate and played a little golf and tennis. They returned to London on their way north to Glamis, where a suite of rooms had been prepared for them (they remained their rooms and they always used them whenever they stayed at Glamis). Unfortunately, the weather was foul – wind, rain and even snow.

The first part of the royal couple's quiet honeymoon was spent at Polesden Lacey, a magnificent Regency house built in 1824, at Great Bookham in Surrey

The changing face of royalty – the Duchess of York at a coconut shy at the Fresh Air Fund Outing at Loughton in July 1923

Not only that, the Duchess had whooping cough – 'Not a very *romantic* disease,' she confided later to a friend.

The little Lady Elizabeth Bowes-Lyon's nickname from the nursery, 'Princess', had come true. No one, least of all the young Duchess of York in that euphoria of courtship, wedding and honeymoon, could have foreseen that, to be truly prophetic, they should have called her 'Queen'.

In his autobiography, *A King's Story*, the Duke of Windsor wrote, 'In 1923 my brother Bertie had married the daughter of a Scottish Earl, Lady Elizabeth Bowes-Lyon, who had brought into the family a lively and refreshing spirit.'

The Duchess of York instantly adapted to her new Royal life, but, at the same time, never lost

The Duke and Duchess of York. The young Duchess bore her new responsibility and title with charm

her own very special brand of tact, warmth and charm. The family loved her for it. At formal dinners at Buckingham Palace and Windsor, it would be the Duchess of York who would put the nervous at their ease; it was she who, as naturally as if she were in the drawing-room at Glamis, would sit down at the piano and sing the popular songs of the day and be joined by other members of the family and guests. George V clung desperately to the nineteenth century and resented any change of habit and manners. He was constantly chaffing at his unmarried sons, especially the Prince of Wales, whose behaviour was an anathema to him. Yet to survive, the Monarchy had to move with the times, to enter the twentieth century. Those close to the Court could see that it was the Duchess of York, with her tact and understanding of the King and his values, who could help make that transition.

It was thought undignified for members of the Royal Family to be seen smiling, let alone laughing, in public. From the start, the Duchess of York was dubbed by the press 'the Smiling Duchess' – her

A stylized portrait of the Duke of York, by Reginald Granville Eves, 1923

A similar portrait by Reginald Granville Eves of the Duchess of York, 1924

other soubriquet was 'the Little Duchess', a reference to her 5 feet 2 inches. The King, a stickler for punctuality, was happy to relax the rules for his daughter-in-law. When she arrived a few minutes late for dinner once, her apology was cut short with, 'Not at all, my dear, we must have sat down a few minutes too early.' The Duchess was at least more punctual than Queen Alexandra, who was even late for her own Coronation.

Soon after they returned from their honeymoon, the King wrote to the Duke of York, 'I am quite certain that Elizabeth will be a splendid partner in your work.' He was right. 'The Foreman', the Prince of Wales's title for his hard-working and conscientious brother, had certainly chosen a bride who would help him in his campaign for better conditions for the working class and industrial relations. Her instant contribution to his work was soon reported by the *Morning Post*:

The Duchess of York. A watercolour painted by Savely Sorine in 1923

At once the Duchess of York bore her rank as if it had been hers by right of birth. She took her place simply and naturally in the ever-expanding public life of her husband. He was especially interested in the social welfare of boys and men; she did similar work among women and girls. While he went over factories and workshops and shipyards, she was unwearied in visiting maternity centres, girls' clubs and housing colonies. They were together all over the United Kingdom and Ulster, crowding their days with beneficent duties, obviously happy in their strenuous work and in each other, and whether she was happier gracing State ceremonies or equipped with a handkerchief drawn over her hair to go down a Durham coal mine, there was no means of determining. That special faction for absorption in the occasion never deserted her.

A French observer at one such ceremony put her appeal more succinctly: 'I suppose Her Royal

The Duchess of York's furniture was removed from 17 Bruton Street to her new home, White Lodge, soon after the wedding

Highness has laid many foundation stones, yet she seems this afternoon to be discovering a new and delightful occupation.' In that one sentence he had pinpointed the unlimited appeal of the Duchess of York, an appeal that has never varied or waned, whatever the occasion, whatever her personal feelings, from those early public engagements to the present day. The Duke of York felt more confident with his wife by his side. Even when they were parted, he had a more assured air and an easier manner with strangers and making speeches.

The Duchess of York's beneficial effect on her husband went far beyond the support that she gave him in his public life. With her love, her unswerving religious faith and confidence and belief *in* him, she became the pivot of his life. She provided that one ingredient that he lacked, something his stiff parents were unable to give, and that was a relaxed and loving home life. It was she who brought out his true potential, who en-

couraged him in difficult times and in conflict. That love and support never faltered in all their married life of almost twenty-nine years, a life so tragically ended with his untimely death in 1952.

That loving 'home life' was fostered in many houses during their marriage. It began at White Lodge, in Richmond Park on the outskirts of London. The house, now the home of the Royal Ballet School, was lent to them as a 'grace and favour' house by the King. It was an unusually difficult task for the newly married Duchess to set up house there for White Lodge was very special to Queen Mary who had been brought up there and had lived there when she herself became Duchess of York. Her eldest child, the Prince of Wales, was also born there.

However, with her usual tact and the experience of setting up 17 Bruton Street, the new Duchess of York managed to make a comfortable home that gained the approval of the Queen, who wrote in her diary, 'She has made the house so very nice with all their presents,' after she and the King lunched there. The Duke had warned by letter, 'I have to warn you that our cook is not

White Lodge in Richmond Park was the Yorks' first home. It had formerly been the home of Queen Mary as a girl and as Duchess of York

very good but she can do the plain dishes well, I know you like that sort.'

The Duchess of York was happy in her new home. She took a particular pride in showing it off to her family and friends, even to a group of Girl Guides from a Dr Barnardo's home who were about to emigrate to Australia. They both enjoyed that first summer at White Lodge, with the lovely views over Richmond Park, the gardens and the new hard tennis court – the Duchess's game was above average thanks to her last governess at Glamis, a Miss Boynard, who was a keen tennis-player. However, with the mists of late autumn the novelty of the house began to wear off and it became increasingly obvious that it was wildly impractical. The house was too large for them and, because of the remoteness, the servants disliked it. It was also too far from London – often they had to drive back from one engagement, change and then return to London for dinner later the same

evening. Above all, it was expensive to run and the central heating was minimal.

During that first summer, there was much travelling. The Duke and Duchess went to Edinburgh with the King and Queen for the reopening of the Palace of Holyroodhouse. While on holiday with the Duchess's sister Rose, at Holwick Hall in Durham, they received a telegram from the King informing them that, for diplomatic reasons, they should leave within three weeks for the Balkans to act as godparents to the heir to King Alexander of Yugoslavia and also to represent the King and Queen at the wedding of Prince Paul of Yugoslavia to Princess Olga of Greece (sister of Princess Marina, who later married the Duke of Kent). Although furious at such a 'request', which meant they had to cut short their holiday, the Duke and Duchess travelled to Belgrade. The Duchess of York was a great success with the European cousins, the Duke writing to his father, 'They were all enchanted with Elizabeth, especially Cousin Missy [Queen Marie of Romania]. She was wonderful with all of them – they were all strangers except two, Paul and Olga.'

The Duke and Duchess of York were much in demand both for ceremonial occasions and to head charitable organizations, especially after the death of Queen Victoria's third daughter, Helen, Princess Christian of Schleswig-Holstein, patron of many institutions associated with nursing and childcare. From those early days she has worked hard for her charities, contributing far more than just her name.

It was not all hard work for the young Duke and Duchess of York. To escape from the cold of White Lodge and to indulge the Duke's new passion for hunting, they took a lease on The Old House at Guilsborough in Northamptonshire for

The Duke and Duchess of York travelled to Yugoslavia in the summer of 1923 to act as godparents to Prince Peter, heir to King Alexander (left). King Ferdinand of Rumania is standing behind Queen Marie who is holding their grandson

the winter. From there, he could hunt with the Pytchley and the Whaddon Chase, while the Duchess could slip down to her family at 'The Bury'. There were also evenings at the theatre – Duff Cooper described them as 'such a sweet little couple, so fond of one another . . . sitting together in the box having private jokes', and there were endless dinner parties and dances.

The problem of White Lodge solved itself in the spring of 1924, when Princess Mary offered her brother and sister-in-law Chesterfield House, her London home, as she had retired to Yorkshire for the birth of her second child. The house came just in time, as that year was to be even more hectic than the previous one. There were State Visits from Romania, Italy and Ethiopia; the British Empire Exhibition at Wembley and a Tour of Northern Ireland as well as many other public engagements up and down the country. Wherever she went, the crowds turned out to see their 'Little Duchess', to

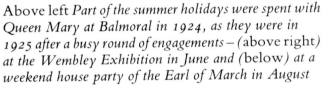

Above left *Part of the summer holidays were spent with Queen Mary at Balmoral in 1924, as they were in 1925 after a busy round of engagements – (above right) at the Wembley Exhibition in June and (below) at a weekend house party of the Earl of March in August*

experience that smile at first hand and possibly a memorable conversation. As the Duke never tired of saying, 'I am very lucky indeed to have her to help me, as she knows exactly what to say to all the people we meet.'

The Duchess had suffered from bronchitis the winter before and the Duke had asked his father for permission to combine an official visit to East Africa and the Sudan with a holiday. Permission was granted and they left on 1 December 1924 by way of Paris and Marseilles, then by liner to Port Said and Mombasa, Kenya's main port, where they arrived three weeks later and were met by the Governor, Sir Robert Coryndon. Then there was a magical journey by train to Nairobi, where they sat for part of the way on a specially constructed platform in front of the engine so that they could see the wildlife. Their official functions over, the Duke and Duchess with their party went on a six-week safari. They travelled through torrential rain and intense heat, but loved every minute of the

The Duchess of York at White Lodge shortly before her departure with the Duke for Africa in December 1924

experience and the African continent. The Duchess, dressed in a khaki bush-shirt, trousers and a floppy hat, went into the bush both to photograph the wildlife and to shoot. She was a good shot, using a Rigby rifle made specially for her (it is now used by her grandson, the Prince of Wales, when stalking at Balmoral). Her trophies were impressive, but her critics were more concerned by the fact that she was enjoying shooting animals rather than that she was shooting endangered species. There was even concern that they themselves were in danger, a far cry from the truth – they were young, healthy and madly happy.

Their safari came to an abrupt end when Sir Robert Coryndon died, and after the funeral they returned home via Uganda, the Sudan and the

The Duchess of York. Painted by Philip de Laszlo, 1925

Nile. It was a wonderful experience, not just as a holiday but as their first contact with the Empire that, in time, was to become the Commonwealth.

Far more daunting for the Duke of York than facing a rhinoceros in the Kenyan bush was the prospect of making a speech in April 1925 at the opening of the Empire Exhibition, of which he had become president. To make it worse, the speech was to be broadcast and to be delivered in front of his father, something that always accentuated his stammer. On the day, the King declared that 'Bertie got through his speech all right,' while others remember that it was 'an agonizing experience to hear him'. The official engagements continued that summer using Curzon House, Lord Curzon's London residence, as a London base, and holidays were spent at Glamis and Balmoral.

The cloud of the death, in November 1925, of the popular and loved Queen Alexandra, the symbol of the Victorian era, had a silver lining. Although it was not announced, it was generally known that the Duchess of York was pregnant.

The Royal Family

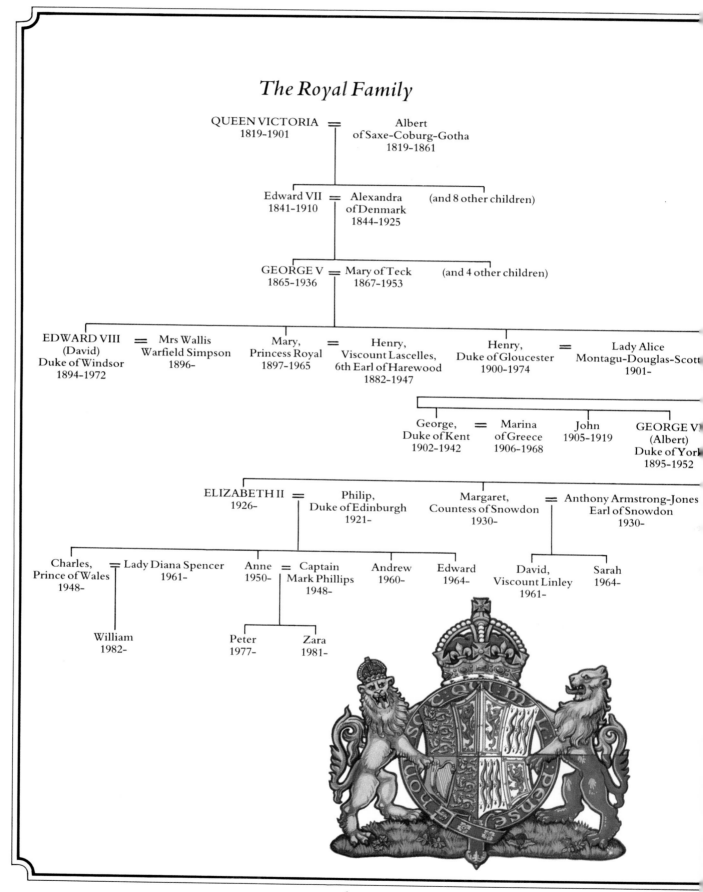

QUEEN VICTORIA 1819–1901 = Albert of Saxe-Coburg-Gotha 1819–1861

Edward VII 1841–1910 = Alexandra of Denmark 1844–1925   (and 8 other children)

GEORGE V 1865–1936 = Mary of Teck 1867–1953   (and 4 other children)

EDWARD VIII (David) Duke of Windsor 1894–1972 = Mrs Wallis Warfield Simpson 1896–

Mary, Princess Royal 1897–1965 = Henry, Viscount Lascelles, 6th Earl of Harewood 1882–1947

Henry, Duke of Gloucester 1900–1974 = Lady Alice Montagu-Douglas-Scott 1901–

George, Duke of Kent 1902–1942 = Marina of Greece 1906–1968

John 1905–1919

GEORGE VI (Albert) Duke of York 1895–1952

ELIZABETH II 1926– = Philip, Duke of Edinburgh 1921–

Margaret, Countess of Snowdon 1930– = Anthony Armstrong-Jones Earl of Snowdon 1930–

Charles, Prince of Wales 1948– = Lady Diana Spencer 1961–

Anne 1950– = Captain Mark Phillips 1948–

Andrew 1960–

Edward 1964–

David, Viscount Linley 1961–

Sarah 1964–

William 1982–

Peter 1977–

Zara 1981–

Family Tree of Queen Elizabeth the Queen Mother

Earls of Strathmore and Kinghorne

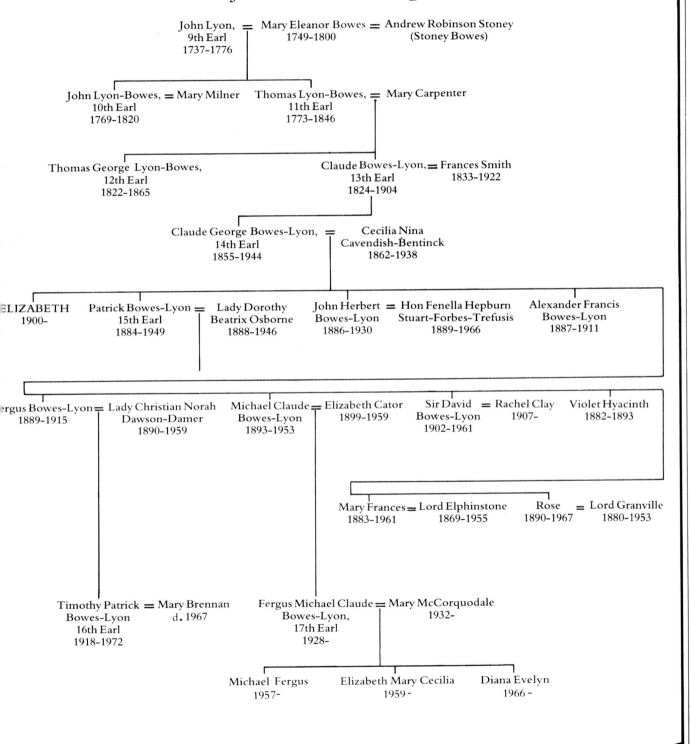

John Lyon, = Mary Eleanor Bowes = Andrew Robinson Stoney
9th Earl   1749-1800   (Stoney Bowes)
1737-1776

John Lyon-Bowes, = Mary Milner   Thomas Lyon-Bowes, = Mary Carpenter
10th Earl   11th Earl
1769-1820   1773-1846

Thomas George Lyon-Bowes,   Claude Bowes-Lyon, = Frances Smith
12th Earl   13th Earl   1833-1922
1822-1865   1824-1904

Claude George Bowes-Lyon, = Cecilia Nina
14th Earl   Cavendish-Bentinck
1855-1944   1862-1938

ELIZABETH   Patrick Bowes-Lyon = Lady Dorothy   John Herbert = Hon Fenella Hepburn   Alexander Francis
1900-   15th Earl   Beatrix Osborne   Bowes-Lyon   Stuart-Forbes-Trefusis   Bowes-Lyon
      1884-1949   1888-1946   1886-1930   1889-1966   1887-1911

rgus Bowes-Lyon = Lady Christian Norah   Michael Claude = Elizabeth Cator   Sir David = Rachel Clay   Violet Hyacinth
1889-1915   Dawson-Damer   Bowes-Lyon   1899-1959   Bowes-Lyon   1907-   1882-1893
      1890-1959   1893-1953   1902-1961

Mary Frances = Lord Elphinstone   Rose = Lord Granville
1883-1961   1869-1955   1890-1967   1880-1953

Timothy Patrick = Mary Brennan   Fergus Michael Claude = Mary McCorquodale
Bowes-Lyon   d. 1967   Bowes-Lyon,   1932-
16th Earl   17th Earl
1918-1972   1928-

Michael Fergus   Elizabeth Mary Cecilia   Diana Evelyn
1957-   1959-   1966-

CHAPTER FOUR

Family Life

The Duke of York wrote to his mother: 'We always wanted a child to make our happiness complete.' A permanent and practical home could also have been added as a postscript. He was determined that he would not spend another winter at White Lodge, or that the baby would be born there but his parents did not sympathize with him. The Duke was about to sign the lease on 40 Grosvenor Square when the Strathmores came to his aid and offered them 17 Bruton Street. Christmas was spent as usual at Sandringham and the Duke and Duchess moved in at the end of January 1926.

The next three months were spent quietly, preparing for the birth of her baby. The Duchess of

A family to complete the Yorks' happiness: left Lander's painting of the Duchess with Princess Elizabeth, 1926 and above with both Princesses, 1934

York 'prised' the invaluable 'Alla' Knight, her old nanny, back from her sister, Lady Elphinstone, who herself had a nine-month-old baby. On the evening of 20 April, the house was milling with people. With the Duchess in her bedroom was the leading obstetric surgeon of the day, Sir Henry Simpson, assisted by Sir George Blacker, Walter Jagger and 'Alla', while below, the Duke waited patiently with his parents-in-law and the Home Secretary, Sir William Joynson-Hicks (known familiarly as 'Jix'), whose presence in the house had been obligatory for 'every birth within the Royal Succession' ever since the 'warming-pan' baby of 1688. At last the waiting was over and it was announced to the newspaper reporters that 'Her Royal Highness, the Duchess of York, was safely delivered of a Princess at 2.40 am this morning, Wednesday, April 21st.' Later the surgeons were to add, 'A certain line of treatment was success-

The Duke and Duchess of York with their first-born, Princess Elizabeth, shortly after her birth

fully adopted.' The Infant Princess, as she was officially known before her christening, was, in fact, born by Caesarean section and in the last bulletin they added that 'The Duchess has had some rest since the arrival of her daughter. Her Royal Highness and the infant Princess are making satisfactory progress.'

It was still raining when the King and Queen drove up from Windsor to see their first grand-daughter, she declaring her 'a little darling with a lovely complexion with fair hair'. The Duke was overjoyed. He wrote to his mother, 'I am so proud of Elizabeth at this moment after all that she has gone through during the last few days and I am so thankful that everything has happened as it should and so successfully. I do hope that you, Papa, are as delighted as we are to have a granddaughter, or would you sooner have had a grandson? I know Elizabeth wanted a daughter. May I say I hope you won't spoil her when she gets a bit older.'

The naming of the infant Princess might have caused a problem, but the King readily approved their choice of 'Elizabeth Alexandra Mary' – E.A.M., the same initials as the Duchess. The King noted, 'He [the Duke of York] says nothing about Victoria. I hardly think that necessary.' It was Queen Victoria's wish that all her male descendants should have the name Albert and the females the name Victoria. As it was thought that the heir to the throne, the Prince of Wales, would marry and produce sons and that the Yorks would have more children, possibly a son, it was likely that the Infant Princess Elizabeth would not stay third in line to the throne for long.

The birth of Princess Elizabeth was largely overshadowed by the General Strike, as was the christening at Buckingham Palace. The Duchess had chosen both grandparents, two sisters, Princess Mary and Lady Elphinstone, and a venerable link with the past, Queen Victoria's third son, the Duke of Connaught, as sponsors – royal god-parents. Despite the efforts of 'Alla' with a bottle of dill water, the baby cried throughout.

The Yorks were to stay at Bruton Street for longer than they expected. They hoped that the King would give them a London establishment, but in the end, the Duke agreed to take the lease of 145 Piccadilly, an austere and dilapidated four-storey terrace house backing onto Hyde Park.

As the house had not been inhabited for six years, there was much to do. In between her multifarious public engagements, the Duchess set about supervising the building works and, later, the décor – mostly pastel shades – and the furnishings. It has been described thus:

The forecourt lay behind iron railings and double black-painted doors led into a short, wide hall with light green pillars, with the dining-room on the left. Beyond the hall, three wide steps led into the morning room which became the most frequently used room in the house. Here dinner parties were occasionally held, if too large for the dining-room, which could only seat twelve. A French window opened onto the private grounds at the rear, Hamilton Gardens, which contained a small lake with mallard, and from here a gate led onto Hyde Park. The drawing rooms were on the first floor with the nurseries at the top of the house, which opened onto a circular gallery under a large glass dome. There was a first-floor balustrade, stone balconies outside the second floor windows, and another balustrade concealing the roof.

It was some time before the Duchess of York was able to move into her London home – not for the more usual reasons of builders' delays but because of a six-month Royal Tour of Australia and New Zealand. The seat of Government of Australia had been moved from Melbourne to the new capital, Canberra, and the Australian Prime Minister, Stanley Bruce, had asked George V if he would send one of his sons to open the new Parliament. The King had no hesitation in informing the Prime Minister that the Duke and Duchess of York would go. It was a brave move as they all

knew how badly the Duke stammered, particularly at important occasions. Since his marriage, his speech had improved slightly and he had learned to avoid words with hard consonants – he never said 'king', but always 'His Majesty' or 'my father'. The Duchess encouraged him, helping him with synonyms that were easier to pronounce. She helped him most when she persuaded her husband to see a new speech therapist who had come to London, Lionel Logue. He was an Australian who had done so well in his home country that he had come to England to set up practice in Harley Street. After the first interview, the Duke really believed that he could be cured. Later, the Duchess went to see him herself so that she, in turn, could understand the treatment and so help her husband. Logue's method of breathing exercises and instilling into his patients the belief that they could be cured worked for the Duke of York and, by the time they were ready to leave for the Royal Tour, the Duke was confident that he would 'not let the side down'.

The Duchess of York was showered with presents, like this teddybear, for her infant daughter, in 1926

The royal couple leave Bruton Street for a tour of Australia and New Zealand on 6 January 1927

The Duchess of York was a devoted mother and, like her own mother, believed that she should be with her child as much as her public engagements would allow. Lady Airlie arrived one day to find her kneeling on the floor with Elizabeth balanced on the sofa:

No doubt about it, a Princess. She was sitting up by herself in the middle of a huge chesterfield, like a white fluff of thistledown. Her hair is very fair and beginning to curl charmingly – owing, the Duchess says, to the untiring attention of her nurse. The baby is always good and she has the sweetest air of complete serenity.

The dreaded day of leaving her sweet and serene daughter came on 6 January 1927. The Duchess wrote to her mother-in-law, 'I felt very much leaving on Thursday, and the baby was so sweet playing with the buttons on Bertie's uniform that it quite broke me up.' The Queen sympathized – twenty-five years before she had made the same tour, leaving her young family. The Duchess at least knew that her daughter was in safe hands with both sets of grandparents.

HMS *Renown* set off from Portsmouth for the round-the-world voyage. Out in the Atlantic, the battle cruiser rolled about like a barrel in the rough weather, and the Duchess proved herself a better sailor than her husband. All was calm when they reached Jamaica. The people went wild to see and meet both the Duke and Duchess. Sadly, the news of the tragic death of the Duchess's friend, Diamond Hardinge, spoiled her enjoyment of the visit. They then travelled on through the Panama Canal and across the Pacific to Fiji, where the Duke saved his wife from the horrors of drinking the local drink, *kava*, a peppery drink made from the kava tree, and then on to New Zealand.

The New Zealanders turned out in their thousands to welcome their Royal visitors to Auckland. The fact that they went there first, as opposed to Australia, particularly pleased the New Zealanders. The tour was strenuous but from the first morning they both coped admirably. The Duke wrote to his mother: 'I had to make 3 speeches the first morning. The last one in the Town Hall quite a long one. I can tell you that I was really pleased with the way I made it, as I had

A game of deck quoits on board HMS Renown *during the tour of Australia and New Zealand*

The Duchess of York found time to fish on South Island during the tour of New Zealand

A rapturous welcome for the Duke and Duchess of York in Auckland, New Zealand, on 1 April 1927

perfect confidence in myself. I did not hesitate at all. Logue's teaching is still working well, but of course if I get tired it still worries me.' From then on, he went from strength to strength.

Those who remember that Royal Tour must surely compare it with the latest tour of the present Prince and Princess of Wales to New Zealand and Australia over fifty years later. They both engendered the same euphoria by their vivid charm, beauty and presence. The task was that much harder for the Duchess as the travelling was then more arduous, the hours longer and her husband was not the 'seasoned campaigner' at Royal Tours that his grandson has become. When the local newspaper wrote: 'She has smiled her way straight into the hearts of the people' they were right.

Crowds gathered at the stations, thronged the streets and lined up at town halls to meet them both. At one station, the Duke of York jumped off

the train and joined the enthusiastic crowd waving and running along the platform beside the Duchess's compartment, much to her amusement. The punishing tour of receptions, dinners, garden parties, balls, speech-making and other official duties continued, with brief fishing expeditions for relaxation. When they reached Christchurch in the South Island the exhausted Duchess fell ill with tonsillitis and had to remain in a hotel in Nelson. The townspeople showered her with flowers she could not smell and fruit she could not eat, although she was naturally grateful for the gifts. Cars were asked to 'Proceed Quietly' and the local paper issued extra editions on her progress. With his deep sense of duty, the Duke, although tempted to remain with his wife, continued the tour on his own. In his typically modest way, he was touched that the crowds came out to cheer him, as he believed that it was the Duchess they wanted to see.

At the end of the tour, they were united aboard the *Renown* and steamed across the 1,200 miles of the Tasman Sea to Australia. In perfect weather, she entered Sydney Harbour, one of the greatest and most beautiful harbours in the world. The Governor General, Lord Stonehaven, wrote to Lord Stamfordham, the King's Private Secretary, of the arrival:

> You can imagine the arrival of the *Renown* in Sydney Harbour on a perfect autumn morning – brilliant sunshine and just enough breeze to blow the flags out. . . . The Harbour was filled with craft of all sorts, which, however, entirely respected the request not to hoot or whistle or make a noise until the anchor was down. The silence added immensely to the impressiveness of the arrival. Once the *Renown* was at anchor the air was made hideous for several minutes by

The highlight of the tour was the opening of the new Federal Parliament in Canberra, 9 May, 1927

all manner of welcoming shrieks and noises – that of course was inevitable.

The cheering and 'welcoming shrieks and noises' went on until the end of the tour two months later. The Australians have always been less formal in their outlook than the New Zealanders and this informality suited the Duke and Duchess. They were 'deeply moved at the personal warmth of their reception and the spirit of devotion to the Crown which they met on every side'. They received sackfuls of mail, mostly inquiring about 'Princess Betty'.

The ANZAC Day ceremonies in Melbourne was one of the most poignant occasions of the whole tour. The march-past of the ex-servicemen from the First World War, some of whom had been at Glamis, was particularly moving for the Duchess as she stood, dressed entirely in black, beside her husband, who took the salute. Among the 25,000

ex-servicemen were forty holders of the Victoria Cross.

The tour of Australia continued at the same hectic pace. Ever mindful of the children who had come to see her, the Duchess requested that the cavalcades should slow down. The headlines in a Queensland newspaper, 'Crowds besiege Duke and Duchess's Car: Unprecedented Scenes: Crowds Out Of Control' became commonplace as they visited each state in turn.

The highlight of the tour was, of course, the opening of the new Parliament on 9 May at Canberra. The Duke, accompanied by the Duchess, unlocked the doors with a golden key and, at his own suggestion, delivered his speech from the steps before entering the building. The speech was broadcast and thousands heard it 'live'. Inside, in

sweltering heat from the lighting, the Duke and Duchess took their respective positions on their thrones, where the Duke made another speech, 'perfectly admirable in delivery'.

A fortnight later they were aboard *Renown* on their way home. The Duke and Duchess were sad to leave Australia, where they had been made so welcome. Sir Tom Bridges, Governor of South Australia, wrote to the King, '. . . the Duchess has had a tremendous ovation and leaves us with the responsibility of having a continent in love with her.'

Only three days out of Australia and four days from Mauritius, the *Renown* ran into trouble. One of the fuel tanks ruptured in the bad weather and the leaking oil caught fire. When the crew had difficulty in putting the fire out, and fearing that the whole ship might blow up if the main tanks caught, the captain, Captain N. Sulivan, ordered the crew to stand by to abandon ship. So as not to

The return of the Duke and Duchess of York to Portsmouth on 27 June 1927 after their successful tour

alarm the Duchess, she was regularly informed that the problem was minor. The fire was finally extinguished and a few days later the Duchess, with her true brand of courage and humour, informed the captain that, 'Every hour someone came and told me that it was nothing to worry about, so I knew there was real trouble.' There were no further incidents on the long voyage home by way of Malta and Gibraltar.

It was a triumphal welcome for the Duke and Duchess of York when they landed on 27 June and were met by the three brothers. The King and Queen came to Victoria Station, but the one person the Duchess really wanted to see was her baby daughter, just fourteen months old. She was frightened that Elizabeth would not recognize her, but she need not have worried. The Queen brought her forward and whispered, 'Look, there's Mummy', and, after a moment's hesitation, she held out her arms to 'be swept into the embrace of the delighted Elizabeth'. The Duke and Duchess of York were truly home.

It was home in every sense of the word. Their new home, 145 Piccadilly, was ready in time for their return, and Elizabeth and 'Alla' had been there for a week already. The weeks after their return were spent by the Duchess in organizing her new home; that they were living in a comparatively modest style compared with other members of the Royal Family – there were no sentries outside the terrace house – was typical of 'the Yorks'. Nor was the twenty-six-bedroomed

The touching family reunion after the six-month parting for the Royal Tour

house too big as all but two of the staff lived in. By today's standards the staff of over twenty was large, but not by comparison with other London houses of the rich. They employed 'a butler, an under-butler, two footmen, a housekeeper, a cook, three housemaids and three kitchenmaids, a nurse and her assistant, a ladies' maid for the Duchess and a valet for the Duke, an odd-job man, a boy who worked in the stewards room, an orderly from the RAF, a night watchman and a telephone operator'.

Above all, 145 Piccadilly was very much a family house. It was just as likely to find Elizabeth's toys scattered over the floor in the morning-room as to meet a Cabinet Minister – most likely both at the same time. Like her mother before her, Elizabeth was to grow up in a wonderful family atmosphere, where strangers were to be charmed, never feared.

While Elizabeth was smuggled out by 'Alla' for a walk in her pram, the Duchess was hard at work. Since the success of the Australian tour, the Duke and Duchess were even more in demand. Theirs was increasingly the 'family image' of Royalty, and they were loved for it. Later, in 1932, two years after the birth of Princess Margaret, the president of the then British College of Obstetricians and Gynaecologists, Sir William Blair-Bell, said of them,

We believe that the sanctity of the family means a great deal to the spiritual and physical welfare of our race. Your Royal Highness has given us all a vision of the happiness of married life, and in a very beautiful way, through the little Princesses, the people have been permitted to share your joys and show their devotion to the Crown.

The failing health of the King, after a bad attack of bronchitis and septicaemia at the base of the right lung in December 1928, increased their burden of those duties, although they never thought of them as a burden; they were at least varied. One day they danced with the pearly kings and queens at the Costermongers' Carnival at Finsbury Town Hall, and on another, the Duchess took up her appointment as Colonel-in-Chief of the first of many regiments, The King's Own Yorkshire Light Infantry, with all that that entailed (including sending the Regiment a Christmas pudding). Deprived children's charities were high on her list of priorities. Forever active, it was

*The Duchess of York and her father-in-law, George V,
were always especially close – seen here with the Duke
of York, Queen Mary, and her daughter Princess
Elizabeth with Alla, at a charity fête at Balmoral, 1927*

she who led the singing in the popular songs of the
day in a festival organized by the Sunshine Guild
of Paddington for 900 children; she who suggested
a visit to a disabled children's hospital in Surrey.
Nor was Scotland forgotten. She was made a
Burgess of the City of Glasgow.

Another Scottish honour was given to the Duke
of York, when, for the first time since James II as
Duke of York in 1679, he was appointed Lord
High Commissioner to the General Assembly of
the Church of Scotland. The opening of the
General Assembly coincided with the 600th
anniversary of the granting of the City Charter of
Edinburgh by their mutual ancestor, Robert the
Bruce. Predictably, their welcome was ecstatic.
The Scotsman reported the next day:

The Duke and Duchess had an ovation infused
with an extraordinary interest and enthusiasm.
The association of the King's son and the little
Duchess who had become the popular darling
of the people transformed the routine welcome
into rapture. . . . Her Royal Highness waved
freely to the crowds, taking special notice of the
children, of whom there were many, and did not
forget to bestow frequent acknowledgements to
spectators in high windows. . . .

The Duchess had learned the trick of picking out
faces in a crowd, giving the impression that the
lucky recipient was the only person there.

Elizabeth was left in London during that
Scottish tour. The Duchess wrote to her mother-
in-law, 'I fear that it has been a very great disappointment to the people, not that they would
have seen her, but they would have liked to feel
that she was here . . . it almost frightens me that the
people should love her so much. I suppose that is a

good thing, and I hope that she will be worthy of it, poor little darling.' Presents were showered on the three-year-old girl (three tons of them from Australia alone, which were later distributed among the needy children of Durham), her clothes and their colours were copied and she was in danger of being mobbed when seen in public. The Duke had commented wryly, 'My chief claim to fame is that I am the father of Princess Elizabeth.'

If the Scots were upset that Elizabeth had not gone to Edinburgh in May 1930, they were more than mollified as the Duchess was determined that her next child was to be born in Scotland. The same team of doctors and surgeons attended the Duchess at Glamis, when it was hoped that the baby would be born on her thirtieth birthday, 4 August. Unfortunately, the baby was not delivered until 21 August, again by Caesarian section. The Labour Home Secretary, Joseph Clynes, sent the customary telegram: 'Yesterday evening at 22 minutes after nine o'clock Her Royal Highness the Duchess of York was safely delivered of a Princess at Glamis Castle.' The three Scottish doctors' addition that 'Her Royal Highness and the Infant Princess are doing fine' was emended to 'doing well' for the English version.

The Duchess's smile charms Glasgow shipyard workers at the launching of the Duchess of York, *1928*

It was no secret that the Duke and Duchess had wanted a son and, with the Bowes-Lyon and Royal Family propensity for producing sons – in that one generation they had produced ten sons to five daughters – they felt certain that it would be a boy and so had no girl's names prepared. The original choice was Ann Margaret, but this was vetoed by the King. The second choice, Margaret Rose, was worded more firmly and given Royal approval.

If all was deliciously happy in the Yorks' house with their now complete family, all was not well with the country. Unemployment rose to its highest level, causing nationwide hardship. The Depression had taken a grim hold, and hunger, poverty and humiliation, all that the Duke and Duchess of York had worked so hard to overcome, were worse than ever. They were deeply conscious of the plight of the people, and did what they could to draw attention to their condition. The only warmth that many saw in those depressed areas was the warmth of the Duchess's smile. Where the King reduced his Civil List (money voted to him by Parliament), the Duke made a small gesture of his own by selling his hunters and giving up hunting.

At that time, a real and lasting pleasure had come into the lives of the Duke and Duchess of York. They had long been looking for a country residence near to Windsor, and when the King offered them Royal Lodge in Windsor Great Park they accepted it instantly and with much excitement. Although it looked shabby, was damp and the recent additions were out of keeping and impractical, the Duchess, with her great imagination, could see the potential. It took nearly a year to restore it so that it was just habitable (other works were delayed until the economic climate of the country improved). Every weekend, the Duke and Duchess escaped with whoever they could muster to work in the garden.

The garden at Royal Lodge was the first of many created by the Duchess. She was continuing a Bowes-Lyon family tradition, and with her artistic skill, eye and knowledge, as well as the Duke's special interest in rhododendrons, she created a garden of exceptional beauty. Whatever time of the year, there is always something of interest, particularly in the spring and early summer, when the Wilderness, a wild garden with its walks through banks of azaleas and

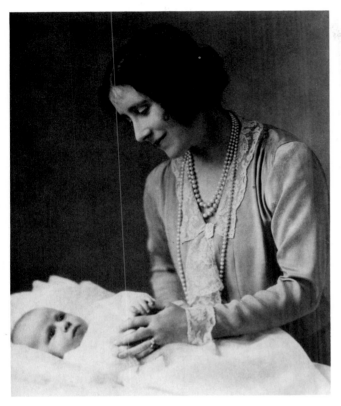

*The Duchess of York with her second daughter,
Princess Margaret, born on 21 August 1930*

*'Three generations' – the Countess of Strathmore, the
Duchess, David Bowes-Lyon and Princess Elizabeth*

rhododendrons, daffodils and primroses, is at its best. Later, Royal Lodge was enlarged with the addition of a nursery wing, larger garages with servants' quarters above and a swimming pool. Today, it is still a wonderful retreat for the Queen Mother, who uses it as often as she can. Another favourite house, Birkhall, on the edge of the Balmoral Estate, was to be lent to the Yorks. This house, too, was considerably enlarged and improved with the Duchess's flair for making her houses comfortable, homely and lived in but, at the same time, grand and in keeping.

An insight into the very private life of the Duke and Duchess of York came from an unexpected quarter. The Duchess taught her daughters in the early stages, reading them Bible stories and grounding them in the three 'R's'. When she suggested that Elizabeth went away to school, the King was horrified, and a governess, a Scots girl called Marion Crawford, later known within the family as 'Crawfie', was engaged. She was to stay with 'the Little Princesses' for fifteen years, and at the end of that time she wrote of her experiences in Royal service. The book was a lucra-

tive indulgence that was ill received in Royal circles. Miss Crawford remembered:

No one ever had employers who interfered so little. I had often the feeling that the Duke and Duchess, most happy in their own married life, were not over-concerned with the higher education of their daughters. They wanted most for them a really happy childhood, with lots of pleasant memories stored up against the days that come and, later, happy marriages.

She told of every detail, from the princesses' morning visit to their parents to the excited bath- and bed-times at night. When their children were tucked up in bed, 'then, arm in arm, the young parents would go downstairs, heated and dishevelled and frequently rather damp. . . . The children called to them as they went, until the door finally closed "Good night Mummie. Good night Papa!"'

It was a blissful existence but one that was almost too good to last. In 1935 the King celebrated his Silver Jubilee, when the nation demonstrated their love and loyalty to their Monarch. The Duke and Duchess of York were very much

George V and Queen Mary with the Royal Family during their Silver Jubilee celebrations in May 1935

part of the celebrations – she was described as 'charming and gracious', the Princesses as 'two tiny pink children'. It was not long before the cheers of the Jubilee celebrations were replaced by the silence of mourning. The King had rallied from his previous illnesses and recovered, but the chill he caught while at Sandringham in January 1936 was to be fatal. The death of the King was to have further-reaching effects than the loss of a loved father, father-in-law and grandfather for the Duke and Duchess of York and their children, as they were to discover, all too soon.

'The King is dead, long live the King.' In one of the most unfortunate reigns in the history of the British monarchy, the idiom was changed not twelve months later to 'The King has gone, long live the King.' After the abdication of Edward VIII, the Prime Minister, Stanley Baldwin, was asked about the Coronation plans. He replied, 'Same date. New King' – the British are a phlegmatic race where their monarchy is concerned.

The Duchess of York was still suffering from a heavy bout of influenza at the funeral of the late King. She wanted to be there, not only to be a support to her husband and elder daughter, but to pay her last respects to a father-in-law who had been very dear to her. On observing the new King standing slightly apart from the rest of his family

in St George's Chapel, Windsor, her lady-in-waiting, Lady Helen Graham, whispered to one of the Household, 'I feel sorry for him. *He* is not going home to a wife behind the tea-pot and a warm fire, with his children making toast for him.' If he had, life for the Duchess of York and her family would have been very different – but, as the world knows, there is no such word as 'if' where history is concerned.

The reign of Edward VIII was heralded with hope for a change. The immensely popular Prince of Wales was young and energetic, and, although he began his reign well enough for the first six months, there were many who were unhappy at the way he cut through most of the traditions of the monarchy. He knew that he could depend on the loyalty, service and friendship of his whole family. For the Duke of York, little had altered since nursery days, when he was happy to follow his extrovert brother. Until then, the brothers had remained close. The favourite Uncle David was always dropping into 145 Piccadilly to see his nieces or driving over from his house, Fort Belvedere in Windsor Great Park, to see them all at Royal Lodge. Sadly, it was not long before the

The Heart of the Empire, 6 May 1935. The Silver Jubilee Service held for King George V and Queen Mary at St Paul's Cathedral. Under the painting's title are the words 'The King Shall Rejoice in Thy Strength O Lord'. From a painting by Frank Salisbury

mentally. I don't know if it is the result of being ill, but I mind things that I don't like more than before.'

Once out of mourning, the pressure was again on the Duchess of York. Queen Mary, stoic in her widowhood, bowed out from public engagements, the Duchess of Kent was busy with her young family and the Duchess of Gloucester was still 'learning the ropes'. Naturally, this extra workload devolved onto the Duchess of York. There were hospitals, schools and playgrounds to open with agricultural shows in the summer – at one, the Royal Show at Bristol, it was so muddy that the Duchess bought herself a pair of willow-calf clogs with sycamore soles to wear. Both the Duke and Duchess showed the acceptable and loved face of Royalty. They visited mines, the Duchess even picking a piece from the coal-face far underground, they went inside miners' cottages and talked to their wives. The Duke went off to his famous boys' camp that he so enjoyed before joining his family at Birkhall in August.

At the same time, in the Mediterranean, there was the other face of Royalty that was less acceptable, the King on holiday. Although the British press were silent on the subject, rumours filtered through from the foreign papers of the King's

'Uncle David', the Prince of Wales, with his neices, Princess Elizabeth and Princess Margaret, at Balmoral during the summer of 1933

The public could easily identify with this family image of the Duke and Duchess of York and their daughters

King, by definition as Sovereign, had distanced himself from the core of his family.

The Court was in full mourning for George V for six months, which meant that all their engagements were cancelled. It also meant that the Duchess of York had more time to devote to her family, but much of that time was spent laid low with influenza. Later, she recuperated at Eastbourne for a month and returned to Royal Lodge for Easter, when Queen Mary joined them for Elizabeth's tenth birthday party and their thirteenth wedding anniversary. She was fully recovered physically after her illness, although, as she admitted to the Royal physician, Lord Dawson, 'I think I am now suffering from the effects of the family break-up, which always happens when the head of the family goes. Though outwardly one's life goes on the same, yet everything is different – especially spiritually and

holiday in the Adriatic. He had chartered a motor yacht, *Nahlin*, and among his guests was a Mrs Wallis Simpson.

She was born Betty Wallis Warfield in Baltimore, Maryland, on the east coast of the United States. The Prince of Wales had first met her in 1931 while spending a weekend near Melton Mowbray, in Leicestershire, hunting with the Quorn. She had recently married Ernest Simpson, a naturalized Englishman and shipping tycoon; both had married for the second time. The Prince of Wales had always been attracted to older, married women, and he met Mrs Simpson again at the house of his current 'older married woman', Lady (Thelma) Furness. From that time onwards, the Simpsons were frequent weekend guests at Fort Belvedere, while the Prince in turn visited them at their London flat. Lady Furness returned to New York for a few months and asked Mrs Simpson to look after her 'little man', as she called the Prince of Wales, while she was away, but Mrs Simpson did more than that. The liaison continued despite open hostility from King George and Queen Mary, who once had to suffer her presence at a ball at Buckingham Palace on the pretext of fostering Anglo-American friendship.

Nor was she any more welcome at Court or in the family after George V died. Once, the young King brought her over to Royal Lodge in his new American station-wagon to show off both to the Yorks. Elizabeth asked, 'Who is *she?*' with a child's sense of occasion. Mrs Simpson later recalled the visit: the Duchess had her 'famous charm' while 'the Duke [was] quiet, shy, obviously dubious of this new-fangled American contrivance . . . While the Duke of York was sold on the American station-wagon, the Duchess was not sold on David's other American interest.'

The more raffish members of the King's friends, who, of course, included Mrs Simpson, and the loyal members of his Household arrived at Balmoral for the summer holidays. For some time the King had distanced himself from his family, particularly the Yorks, and he had often instructed his brother to carry out the more unpopular of the economies on the Royal estates and within the Household. It was some time before the Yorks were asked over to Balmoral from Birkhall for dinner. It can only have been galling for the Duchess to see Mrs Simpson acting as hostess rather than being just one of the guests (the Duke

Edward VIII seen here with Mrs Simpson at Balmoral in 1936. What the press dubbed as 'the King's Affair' led to his abdication

was upset at being commanded to fill in for the King at the opening of a hospital in Aberdeen while he met Mrs Simpson at the local railway station). It was not that she made him especially happy either – her carping and criticism seemed to go unnoticed by the King. No wonder the Court was whispering, 'King Edward the Eighth and Mrs Simpson the seven-eighths.'

Matters that the press were later to dub 'The King's Affair' began to accelerate. Mrs Simpson obtained a divorce from her husband at the end of October, and she would therefore be free to marry in six months' time, two weeks before the Coronation set for 12 May 1937. The thought of a twice-married woman with two husbands still living being married to the King, the Defender of the Faith, was unthinkable. There were, however, three courses open to them. Mrs Simpson could go away, the King could abdicate if he wanted to marry her (which he chose), or they could contract a morganatic marriage, whereby they could marry but she would not have the status of Queen. The Prime Minister, Stanley Baldwin, told the King firmly there was no precedent for a morganatic marriage, and that if he was adamant in marrying Mrs Simpson, the Government would resign.

The weeks leading up to what seemed unthinkable but becoming more and more likely, the Abdication, were a total nightmare for the Duke and Duchess of York. All that the Duchess had feared when she refused the Duke's first proposal was now not only coming true but was far worse as she faced the possibility of becoming Queen Consort. All that she feared for her family was about to become a reality. George V had seen it, and shortly before he died, he said to Baldwin, 'After I'm dead, the boy will ruin himself in twelve months.' One last wish was also

Crowds gathered outside the Duke and Duchess of York's home at 145 Piccadilly as the constitutional crisis worsened after the attack on the King by the press early in December 1936

answered – that his 'eldest son will never marry and have children, and that nothing will come between Bertie and Lilibet [Princess Elizabeth] and the Throne'. Where the old King wished it, the Duchess of York feared it most of all.

On 1 December 1936, while the Duchess of York was receiving the Freedom of the City of Edinburgh, the Bishop of Bradford made a speech (he says unintentionally) that attacked the King's relationship with Mrs Simpson. This gave the press the opportunity for which they had been waiting. They reported the speech and wrote their leaders on it. Once the story was out, they attacked the King, saying that the monarchy was more important than the present incumbent. As Mrs Simpson left for France, the street carol singers had added another couplet to the carol:

> Hark the herald angels sing
> Mrs Simpson's pinched our King.

From then on, it was a countdown to the day, 11 December, when the ex-King sailed to France. On 3 December, the Duke and Duchess of York

returned to London and the headlines in the newspapers, 'The King's Marriage'. The Duke of York drove straight to Marlborough House to see his mother, where he met the King, who declared that he was going to marry Mrs Simpson and that he could not live without her. He asked the Duke to come and see him at Fort Belvedere the next day. The Yorks spent the weekend waiting for the summons from the King, which finally came on the Monday evening, 7 December. The King then told his brother, the Heir Presumptive, that he was determined to abdicate. The next night, the Duke, his brother the Duke of Kent, Stanley Baldwin and Walter Monckton, the King's aide, dined with the King, when all the details were worked out. The strain over the last few weeks for the Duke and Duchess had been immense and the Duchess went down with a bad attack of influenza. She desperately wanted to be at her husband's side in the crisis, but the doctors forbade it, keeping him, tired and vulnerable, away from her.

On 10 December, the King's abdication was signed and witnessed by his three brothers in the drawing-room of Fort Belvedere. At lunch the following day, a telephone call came from the House of Lords, where 'His Majesty's Declaration of Abdication Bill' had just been ratified, 'Will you tell his Majesty that he has just been proclaimed King?' Sir Eric Miéville took the message to the dining-room, where the family were lunching. King George VI looked around the table and asked, 'Now if someone comes through on the telephone, *who* shall I say I am?' A fine spark of humour in such an anxious time. That night the ex-King broadcast to the nation:

At long last I am able to say a few words of my own. I have never wanted to withhold anything but until now it has not been constitutionally possible for me to speak. A few hours ago I discharged my last duty as King and Emperor, and now that I have been succeeded by my brother, my first words must be to declare my allegiance to him. This I do with all my heart.

You all know the reasons which have impelled me to renounce the throne, but I want you to understand that in making up my mind I did not forget the country or the Empire, which as Prince of Wales and lately as King I have for twenty-five years tried to serve. But you must believe me when I tell you that I have

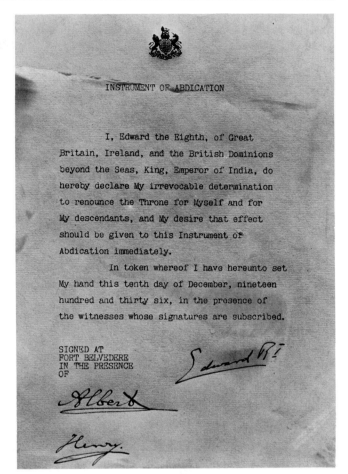

Edward VIII's Instrument of Abdication that led to the succession of the Duke of York as King George VI

found it impossible to carry the heavy burden of responsibility and discharge my duties as King as I would wish to do without the help of the woman I love. . . .

This decision has been made less difficult to me by the sure knowledge that my brother, with his long training in public affairs of this country and his fine qualities, will be able to take my place forthwith without interruption or injury to the life and progress of the Empire. And he has one matchless blessing, enjoyed by so many of you and not bestowed on me, a happy home with his wife and children. . . .

And now we have a new King, I wish him and you, his people, happiness and prosperity with all my heart. God bless you all. God save the King.

That night the ex-King boarded HMS *Fury* and sailed for France and exile.

CHAPTER FIVE

Queen Consort

The Queen wrote in a 'long and delightful letter' to her friend Dr Cosmo Lang, then Archbishop of Canterbury: 'I can hardly now believe that we have been called to this tremendous task and (I am writing to you quite intimately) the curious thing is that we are not afraid. I feel God has enabled us to face the situation calmly.' She signed the letter, 'for the first time and with great affection, Elizabeth R'.

Although the King feared that he would be confused with his father, he informed the Privy Council that he had decided to adopt the title of George VI. The name at least would promote a sense of continuity in the monarchy. The British monarchy had suffered a terrible shock, the Abdication might have wrecked it. However, taking a retrospective view of the personalities involved, it is more than likely that the change of kings actually saved it. The mercurial Edward VIII

was replaced by a man who was his antithesis, dedicated, gentle and cautiously progressive, whose transparent good qualities and faith were to restore the Crown. The new King also knew where his strength lay. In a tense speech, he told the Council, 'With my wife and helpmate by my side, I take up the heavy task which lies before me.' The day after, the King's forty-first birthday, he conferred the most senior Order, the Order of the Garter, on the Queen, just as his father had done for Queen Mary on his birthday.

The press also knew where much of the King's strength lay. The *Morning Post* wrote of her: 'She industriously and faithfully gives her services to as many good causes as it is possible for her to help, living laborious days, never sparing herself and

An early study of the new King and Queen Consort from the Illustrated London News, *15 May 1937*

Still very much a mother, the Queen with her daughters in December 1936

doing it all with such a happy goodwill that she is considered patroness and very sincere friend.' *The Times* went further, saying that she was 'all the public had hoped for . . . the heart of the nation had warmed towards the gracious Scottish girl with beauty of feature and complexion, a low-toned charming speaking voice, and above all a particularly happy and even radiant expression'.

There is normally a period of six months mourning on the accession of a new monarch, giving time to acclimatize to the position. With George VI and his Queen Consort, there was no such luxury, although the traditional Christmas break at Sandringham allowed them a little relaxation and a chance to review their new positions. Just as the young Lady Elizabeth Bowes-Lyon slipped easily into the role of Duchess of York, so the Duchess became Queen. Over the next few months she was to become 'Queenly' –

although nothing in her personality altered, least of all her 'delicious smile', she walked more slowly and with greater dignity, the spontaneous enthusiasm of her wave to the crowds was more regal and her wardrobe dictated less to the fashion of the day but to 'what was most suitable for the occasion'. The transformation merely enhanced her value to the nation and particularly to the King.

The next great change, which was to affect the little Princesses as much as their parents, was the move to Buckingham Palace from their 'cosy home' at 145 Piccadilly. The Palace, with its 600 rooms, was a barracks of a place, cold, impersonal and, as Queen Mary had removed her famous collection of furniture to her new home at Marlborough House, largely unfurnished. The Queen immediately set about preparing a few rooms for her family to live in in reasonable comfort and homeliness – what she could not achieve in immediate décor was made up with flowers, family photographs and loved and familiar objects scattered around. The King always maintained that she could 'make a home anywhere'. To Elizabeth, the vermin-man, who was employed

full-time to keep the mouse population down to an 'acceptable level', was the worst part of moving in.

The Coronation of Edward VIII had been set for 12 May 1937 and there seemed no reason to alter it for George VI – the only change was the welcome addition of a Queen Consort. Although seeming a long time, five months was hardly long enough to complete the new preparations. The original dress made by the faithful Handley Seymour for the Duchess of York needed only small alterations to transform it for the Queen Consort. It was 'of white satin cut on the cross, according to the thirties fashion, and again embroidered with the national emblems [both the British Isles and the Dominions] in glittering diamanté. The Queen's personal choice showed in her white satin shoes with their high heels – a style from which she has never deviated – adorned with oak leaves and thistles of England and Scotland in gold thread.' As is traditional with every Queen Consort, a new crown had to be made for her by the Court jewellers, in which, among other priceless gems, was the fabulous Koh-i-Noor diamond, the 'Mountain of Light'. Her Coronation robes, modelled on those of Queen Alexandra, combined a cape of

Now in direct line to the throne, the lives of the Princesses changed greatly

A crown for the Scottish consort – it included the Koh-i-Noor diamond from Queen Mary's crown

ermine and a train of Royal purple velvet that was eighteen feet long. Like the dress, it was embroidered with the emblems of the British Isles and ten of the Dominions. The dresses and robes of Elizabeth and Margaret were identical, the robes being of purple velvet and exact copies of Queen Mary's robes when she had attended the Coronation of Edward VII as Princess of Wales. The up-and-coming designer Norman Hartnell was asked to design the dresses for the six maids-of-honour.

The great day of the Coronation dawned wet and cold. The King and Queen had been woken long before dawn by the loudspeakers being tested. He was so nervous that he could not eat breakfast, but, to their delight, Elizabeth presented them with an essay she had written in red crayon entitled, 'The Coronation, 12 May 1937. To Mummy and Papa. In memory of their Coronation, from Lilibet By Herself.' The King and Queen left in the State Coach for Westminster Abbey through cheering crowds at exactly half-past ten. They were preceded by Queen Mary and the little Princesses. Queen Mary broke the

tradition of a dowager queen not attending a Coronation in order to show family solidarity, and the young Princesses' popular appearance emphasized that it was very much the Coronation of the Royal *Family*.

At the Abbey, the King and Queen waited in the robing room before the Queen's procession moved off in great splendour. One of the Household was later to record, 'I think that her Coronation Day was the first time I recognized this unusual quality which Queen Elizabeth has for drawing all eyes to her, so you do not notice that other people are present at all. The Duchess of Northumberland [the Queen's Mistress of the Robes, who followed closely in her procession] is a fine-looking woman, yet we never looked at her. Queen Mary looked so majestic that when she entered I feared that she would completely over-shadow the younger woman, yet that was not so.'

The King's procession went off without mishap although, as he recorded in his diary that night, 'the white . . . surplice which the Dean of Westminster insisted I should put on was inside out'; when the time came to take the Coronation Oath, the 'Bishop could not find the words so the Archbishop held his book down for me to read, but horror of horrors his thumb covered the words of the Oath'. He was also worried that the crown was

The Coronation of Their Majesties King George VI and Queen Elizabeth, 12 May 1937 – the queen as yet uncrowned. Painted by Frank Salisbury

THE CROWNING OF THE QUEEN·CONSORT: THE ARCHBISHOP PLACING THE CROWN UPON HER MAJESTY'S HEAD.

After the ceremonies of the King's Crowning had been completed, Queen Elizabeth rose from her Chair of State and went to the Altar, supported by two Bishops and attended by her ladies and pages. She knelt there during the Prayer of Consecration, and at a faldstool set before the Altar for her Anointing and Crowning. During the Anointing four Duchesses held above her a Canopy of cloth of gold, just as the four Knights of the Garter had held one over the King. The Archbishop set the Ruby Ring on the fourth finger of her right hand, and, taking the Crown from the Altar, placed it upon her head. The Queen's Crown, designed for the occasion, is the first entirely mounted in platinum. Among its jewels—all diamonds— is the Koh-i-Noor, which was also set in Queen Mary's Crown in 1911.

FROM THE PAINTING BY FORTUNINO MATANIA, R.I.

on the right way round – a small red thread of cotton marking the front had been removed and, 'as I turned after leaving the Coronation chair, I was brought up all standing, owing to one of the bishops treading on my robe. I had to tell him to get off it pretty sharply. . . .'

The King crowned, it was the turn of the Queen. As she moved from the Chair of Estate she glanced at the Royal Box containing her daughters, her parents, Queen Mary and the Princess Royal, (Princess Mary) and other senior members of the Royal Family. After she was crowned and anointed by the Archbishop of Canterbury at the altar steps, she returned to her throne, where she and the King received Holy Communion. The service over, the King and Queen returned to Buckingham Palace. The route they took formed

Left *The crowning of the Queen Consort. From a painting by Fortunino Matania*
Right *The King and Queen in the Golden State Coach return to Buckingham Palace on Coronation Day*
Below *One of the five balcony appearances – this one with Queen Mary (centre), Princess Elizabeth (left) and Princess Margaret*

*Opposite Coronation Glory – the Royal Family in
Coronation robes and crowns, 12 May 1937*

a great loop – from Parliament Square they processed along the Embankment, then up Northumberland Avenue to Trafalgar Square, down Pall Mall and up St James's, then right into Piccadilly and up Regent's Street to Oxford Street. At Marble Arch, they turned south down Park Lane to Hyde Park Corner, then down Constitution Hill to the Palace gates. They were cheered every inch of the way; some had waited in the rain and cold all night. At Hyde Park Corner, the procession was televised by the first ever outside broadcast of the BBC (although the newsreel cameras and BBC Radio were allowed to record and broadcast the service, television cameras were banned from the Abbey).

As the newly crowned King and Queen made their five balcony appearances at Buckingham Palace, the crowd surged forward and cheered. In a classic understatement, the Queen is said to have murmured, 'They seem to like us.'

The tremendous success of the Coronation was followed by tours of London – three in all and not all of them planned. Their Daimler was mobbed wherever they went by cheering crowds, who enthusiastically welcomed their Sovereign and his Queen Consort. It seemed that the ghost of 'The King's Matter' had been laid. In fact, behind the scenes, there was more anguish, as the King had conferred on his brother the title of Duke of Windsor and, by Letters Patent, the form His Royal Highness. Although after their marriage Mrs Simpson became the Duchess of Windsor, she was definitely not to be styled 'Her Royal Highness'. Later, photographs of the Duke and Duchess of Windsor being received by Adolf Hitler were to distress many more than just the King and Queen.

The London visits were followed by the customary review of the Fleet at Spithead and tours of Wales, Scotland and Northern Ireland. The Northern Irish were just as ecstatic. The King made a speech in the Belfast Council Chamber, and when they left the local paper commented:

At his [the King's] side was the smiling and radiant Queen, whose grace and charm, added to splendid qualities of mind and heart, have enthroned her in the affections of the whole

Empire. Their Majesties have now completed their round of Coronation visits, by means of which they have not merely heightened their personal popularity but have made the throne even more securely founded upon the solid basis of constitutional usage and popular assent.

The King and Queen stepped up their campaign for better housing for the poor, she frequently making sorties into deprived areas, calling unexpectedly on any house to look over it. One housewife remarked, 'She chatted to me as if she was my neighbour from over the fence' – she was the Queen, but she still had the 'common touch' and she was loved the more for it.

As the Queen was making her presence felt throughout the British Isles, Hitler was becoming a threat to peace with his massive rearmament. For the Queen, there was a more immediate and

Although Elizabeth was now Heir Presumptive the Queen took care to dress her daughters alike

Queen Elizabeth – loyal wife, devoted mother and gracious Queen. A painting by Sir Gerald Kelly

private tragedy within the family. Her mother, Lady Strathmore, was seriously ill. Despite her many engagements, the Queen found time to visit her often in her nursing home. She died at the end of June 1938 with most of her family, including the King, present. It was a terrible blow for the whole family and friends, especially the Queen. The Archbishop of Canterbury in his address at the memorial service put it succinctly when he said, 'She raised a Queen in her own home, simply by trust and love, and as a return, the Queen has won widespread love.'

The State Visit to France of the King and Queen was postponed for three weeks due to Lady Strathmore's death. The Queen's entire wardrobe, a bright and colourful collection based on the Winterhalter paintings of the Empress Eugénie and the Empress Elizabeth of Austria in Buckingham Palace – the idea was the King's – had been designed by Norman Hartnell. But the Queen now had to wear mourning and the colours were no longer appropriate until Hartnell suggested to the King that white was 'a royal prerogative for mourning'. In the remaining two weeks before the start of the tour the most important dresses were made up in white.

The State Visit, including the effect of the Queen's new clothes all in white, was a phenomenal success. For the four days of the visit, France reverted to a monarchy and the French press remarked, 'We have taken the Queen to our hearts. She rules over two nations.' While their visit provided a brief ray of sunshine in France, Hitler's war clouds had already gathered over eastern Europe. By September, Germany had marched into Czechoslovakia and the war that had seemed inevitable was suddenly averted by the Prime Minister, Neville Chamberlain, who negotiated a worthless agreement with Hitler. His famous phrase, 'Peace in our Time', was to be short-lived. The annual summer holiday at Balmoral was punctuated with the King's dashes to London as the situation worsened.

That winter, Britain went into a full rearmament programme. The King and Queen visited naval dockyards and launched warships where they had formerly launched liners, although the Queen did launch the massive Cunard liner, *Queen Elizabeth*, the largest ship in the world, in Glasgow. They visited armaments factories and civil defence installations as well as hospitals. And their planned visit to Canada and the United States in the summer of 1939 still went ahead.

The only change to the schedule was that, so as not to tie up the valuable battle cruiser HMS

The Queen's wardrobe by Norman Hartnell was much admired in Paris during the State Visit in July 1938

Lifeboat drill – on board the Empress of Australia *during the voyage to Canada, 1939*

Repulse in which the Atlantic crossing was to have been made, the King and Queen used a chartered liner, the *Empress of Australia*. The voyage was a nightmare and was described by the Queen in a letter to Queen Mary: 'For three and a half days we only moved a few miles. The fog was so thick that it was like a white cloud round the ship . . . we nearly hit a [ice-] berg the day before yesterday....' Later, when asked if it were not terrible, the Queen replied, 'Yes, it was. You see, we lost two days of the tour.' The King was merely grateful for the extra rest.

When they arrived in Canada, they were met by the Governor-General, Lord Tweedsmuir (better known as the novelist John Buchan). From the moment of their arrival, the Queen threw herself, almost literally, into the tour. She dived into crowds and she talked to everyone, especially the children. The French Canadians were won over by the Queen who made speeches in French. It was a strenuous tour, almost 5,000 miles by rail and boat, but the King and Queen insisted that they visit every state rather than attend a few rarefied receptions in the capital, Ottawa. Outback villages of a few hundred people swelled to crowds of over 20,000 and more crowds gathered along the tracks on raised platforms – some five miles long – wherever their train passed. Once, in the middle of the night, the driver of the train signalled back that there was a crowd ahead. The Queen, dressed in a warm coat and jewellery, stood on the observation platform of the carriage to be 'seen' as the train inched its way through the throng. The Queen was not going to disappoint anyone.

In June 1939, the King and Queen went on to the United States of America. They were uncertain of their reception, but they need not have worried. Their tour had far-reaching political implications as the American President, Franklin D. Roosevelt, knew full well. He hoped, and succeeded, to foster Anglo-American unity, so that if his country was drawn into the war, as surely it

Left and above *The State Visit to the United States of America. The procession to the White House in July 1939 – the Queen accompanied by Mrs Roosevelt, the President's wife, in the first car. Despite the heat wave that gripped Washington, the crowds turned out to welcome the King and Queen*

must be, then the Americans would at least have better contact with her allies. The tour did much to restore a hitherto lukewarm American affection for Britain. The phenomenal heat of Washington did nothing to lessen the ardour of their welcome; the newspaper headlines ran: 'The British re-take Washington.' In New York the crowds were just as ecstatic, and showed their appreciation during the traditional motor-cavalcade. They dubbed the Queen the 'Fairy Queen' and voted her 'Woman of the Year'. One magazine reported: 'The Queen is a beautiful woman, with a complexion that would knock them dead in Hollywood. Her smile, when she lets

go, as she does frequently, is best of all.' The tour ended with a brief but informal stay with the Roosevelts at their home, Hyde Park. The tour was described as a 'triumph'; it is impossible to gauge exactly how much American support to Britain in the vital war years can be attributed to that tour, but safe to say, 'not a little'.

The King and Queen returned to Canada for just four days before sailing home. After the thirty-day tour, a lady-in-waiting mentioned that, 'The Queen was really exhausted by the time we left for home. But she would never say she found anything tiring, and she always brushed off any reference to her fatigue.' They had loved the Canadians, who in return had loved them. Both were sorry when they left. The Queen ended a broadcast: '. . . this wonderful tour of ours has given me memories that the passage of time will never dim. . . .' When they arrived home, the King modestly felt of the tour, 'This has made us' – as if they were not made before.

CHAPTER SIX

War and Peace

There is no school for Royalty, no course in 'kingship', yet throughout history all the members of the Royal Family have had to find their own level, to make their own mark. For King George VI and Queen Elizabeth there were no half-measures. They led from the front, without regard for their own personal safety; like many of their fellow countrymen, their home was bombed and they suffered the wartime shortages and discomfort alongside their people.

With the outbreak of the Second World War, the Queen had an extra role in life, besides that of wife of the Sovereign and mother of her daughters. Where the King was titular head of the three services, busy at home and overseas, the Queen was to lead the battle on the home front. It was a leadership through example, not just by words, although her wartime broadcasts gave hope and comfort to millions at home and abroad. In all, the King and Queen were to travel over half a million miles by road and in the Royal Train, visiting the worst-stricken areas of the Blitz – often just after the raid, with the houses still blazing. It was no coincidence that crowds gathered outside Buckingham Palace in times of peril as well as in victory. The courage and faith of the King and Queen were an inspiration to the people, who drew strength and hope from their combined leadership.

War was finally declared on 3 September 1939, two days after Hitler invaded Poland. The King was in London, the Queen at Balmoral with

On New Year's Eve, 1939, the King broadcast to the nation, 'I said to the man who stood at the gate of the Year, "Give me a light that I may tread safely into the unknown." And he replied, "Go out into the darkness and put thine hand into the hand of God. That we shall be to thee better than light and safer than a known way."

The King and Queen constantly sought to raise the nation's morale – visiting air-raid shelters in 1939

Elizabeth and Margaret before returning to be with her husband. A friend commented, 'I have never seen the Queen more closely resemble her mother, Lady Strathmore, than she did in those first days of the war. She was a tower of strength.' She visited Civil Defence installations, anti-aircraft batteries and saw evacuees leaving for the country and in their new homes. Later, she was to send a card to all who had taken in evacuees to show her appreciation of their selflessness. She inspected units of the Red Cross and the St John Ambulance Brigade and became the Commander-in-Chief of the three women's services, the WRNS, the ATS and the WAAF.

The period of what was to be known as the 'phoney war' – the first eight months – was soon over and the invasions Hitler had promised began. Elizabeth and Margaret came south from Balmoral for a family Christmas at Sandringham, but in the New Year it was thought prudent to send them to Windsor Castle for safety against possible abduction. An offer came from the Canadians for the Princesses to join the thousands of evacuee children in the safety of the Dominion, but the Queen thanked them and declined their offer with, 'The Princesses could never leave without me, and I could never leave without the King and – of course – the King will never leave.'

The German army began its advance through Europe and on 9 April invaded Denmark and Norway. It was only a matter of weeks before France, the Netherlands, Luxembourg and Belgium followed. Buckingham Palace became a refuge for the crowned heads of Europe, too – Queen Wilhelmina and her family from the also been forgiven for his part in the Abdication. The Duke and Duchess of Windsor had returned from exile at the start of the war, but, after a spell in the Embassy in Paris, they ended up away from England, he as Governor of the Bahamas.

As the invasion became imminent the King and Queen reluctantly took to a bullet-proof car whenever they travelled and were always armed – the Queen carrying a small .38 revolver, maintaining that 'I shall not go down like the others'. They carried steel helmets and gas-masks, the Queen having a specially large handbag to carry hers.

In the September of 1940, the Blitz began with a massive bombing of London. A delayed-action bomb landed at Buckingham Palace and exploded the next day, 10 September, shattering the windows on the north side. Three days later, a bold Luftwaffe pilot flew over London in a low raincloud, up The Mall and dropped a stick of six bombs directly on the Palace, completely destroying the Chapel. It was only revealed after the war how close to death, and in what danger, the King and Queen lived. In all, the Palace was hit nine times. One of the Household was to record, 'The King did not mind bombs, he was as brave as a lion, it was only the irritations that could upset him, and the Queen was magnificent, she was without physical fear. And she utterly ignored the possibility that anyone else might feel less brave.'

After each bombing, the King and Queen drove to the worst areas. The Queen was to say, 'I'm glad we've been bombed, it makes me feel I can look the East End in the face.' On one such visit, the air-raid warning sounded and the King and Queen dived into the nearest shelter to the intense delight of the East End occupants. They were offered chairs and strong tea and heard at first hand how much they were appreciated. Sometimes the sights were horrendous, but the Queen had exactly the right word of comfort, never once showing a tell-tale sign of emotion. 'All the people loved her for being there and for looking smiling and serene. They used to say that cliché continually, "Isn't she lovely?"'

An unfinished portrait of Queen Elizabeth by Augustus John, 1940. The sittings at Buckingham Palace were postponed at the start of the Blitz, but when she offered to sit again in 1942, the artist had shut the canvas away. It was presented to the Queen Mother shortly after his death in 1961

A family photograph at Windsor Castle on the fourteenth birthday of Princess Elizabeth, 1940

Netherlands, King Haakon and his family from Norway and King Zog and Queen Geraldine after the Italians had invaded Albania. The Queen saw to it that they had everything they needed in the most tactful way, as her royal guests had arrived with nothing apart from what they stood up in.

At Dunkirk, on 3 June 1940, over 350,000 British and nearly 140,000 French troops were 'plucked' off the beaches. Certain defeat was turned into a victory for the Royal Navy and the civilian fleet. The Queen was immensely proud of the evacuation, just what she would have expected from 'the great British people'.

Britain, under her new Prime Minister, Winston Churchill, had its back to the wall, and the threat of invasion grew daily. Mr Churchill was to become a close friend of the King and Queen – where former and later Prime Ministers were entered in the King's diary by their surname only, it was not long before he was just 'Winston'. He had

The King and Queen with Winston Churchill inspect bomb damage at Buckingham Palace in September 1940 – the Palace was hit nine times in all

Although she tried to spend the nights at Windsor Castle with her daughters, the Queen could not always return. Sometimes she was out of London on the Royal Train, visiting other stricken areas such as Coventry, Bristol, Birmingham and the North, Wales and Scotland. It was a trail of human suffering, of misery and hardship, but wherever the Queen went she left behind a legacy of warmth, understanding and sympathy. Later, a tribute was paid to her, 'During the full weight of the enemy attack on London, the Queen became a shining symbol of her sex. Wherever the bombs fell thickest, there she was to be found bringing comfort and encouragement to the homeless.' It was not just London where her presence was felt, the same could be said of every blitzed area in the country. On one occasion in a badly bombed part of London she was able to coax, with her soft and gentle voice, a terrified terrier out of the rubble, 'I have a way with dogs,' she said. On another occasion she was to coax a deserter out of his predicament when he sneaked into the Queen's bedroom one evening at Windsor Castle. When she entered the room he threw himself at her feet and grabbed her ankles. The Queen later wrote, 'For the moment my heart stood absolutely still.' Then she said, 'Tell me about it.' Her soothing voice calmed him and, as he poured out his 'sad tale', the Queen was able to summon help.

One common feature of the visits to bombed areas was that the Queen always dressed up. 'If the poor people came to see me,' she said, 'they would wear their best clothes.' Norman Hartnell designed a range for her in light pastel colours in lilacs, pinks and pale blues that would not show the dust of a bomb site in the way that darker colours would. Although not superstitious, she never wore black or green in case she met someone who was.

The contribution of the Queen to the war effort went far beyond the invaluable visits to stricken areas and visits to the wounded in hospitals; when she visited the munitions factories,

Above *All through the war the King and Queen
visited bombed areas giving comfort to stricken families
– here in south London, September 1940* Right
*Princesses Elizabeth and Margaret spent most of the
war years at Windsor Castle where lessons went on
as normal – here in the gardens, 1941*

production dropped on the day of the visit as she
talked to as many people as possible, then it soared
on the days following. The first 'Queen's Mes-
sengers', as the convoys of food to the badly
bombed cities became known after her patronage
and financial support, were sent on their way by
the Queen with, 'The message which I would
entrust to these convoys will not be one of encouragement, for courage is never lacking in the
people of this country. It will be rather one of true
sympathy and loving kindness.' She broadcast to
the women of France after their country had
fallen, and it may be that her broadcast to the
United States of America (to thank them for the
food parcels) had some influence on the crucial
talks between Churchill and Roosevelt about

*The Royal Family 1942 – they remained a constant
source of strength to the nation. The King and Queen
travelled thousands of miles visiting devastated areas*

America entering the war. Certainly it must have
reached the hearts of the Americans; whenever
newsreels showed her on the screen, an involuntary
cheer went up in the cinema.

The Times reported the speech, and in its leader
accurately summed up the Queen's position:

The true import of these phrases is that when the
Queen speaks of and for the working women of
Britain, she has every right to speak as herself
being one of them. Very little of her ceaseless
activity gets into the newspapers. It is impossible
to put into print the qualities of head and heart
which give a vitalizing power to her public life.

Soon after America joined the Allies, Mrs
Roosevelt went to stay at Buckingham Palace.
Not even with the visit of the First Lady of the
United States, and a friend at that, did the wartime
strictures at Buckingham Palace improve, nor was

An informal portrait at Royal Lodge, Windsor, 1942

the heating stepped up (Eleanor Roosevelt had a single-bar electric fire in the bedroom the Queen had generously vacated) – 'Buckingham Palace is an enormous place and without heat,' she was to write. A line was painted around the bath, five inches from the bottom, which was the depth of water allowed. The food was pure canteen fare, but served on gold or silver plate.

The King was determined to visit the victorious troops in North Africa and flew to see them in June 1943. The journey was a hazardous one, not least the bad weather over Gibraltar, and the Queen worried over the safety of the King. But all was well and the visit a success. For the first time, the Queen deputized at an investiture at the Palace, decorating, among others, the 'Dam Busters' for their raid with bouncing bombs on the Moehne and Eder dams. She awarded Wing Commander Guy Gibson the Victoria Cross.

During that time, and with her multifarious self-appointed duties, the Queen devoted as much time as possible to her children. Many a night was

The park and golf course at Sandringham were ploughed up and cultivated to help the war effort. Inspecting the harvest during petrol rationing in 1943

spent with them in the bomb shelter at Windsor Castle and every spare moment of the day she tried to be with them too. She well remembers her own wartime childhood at Glamis Castle and could doubly sympathize with her daughters being virtual prisoners at Windsor. When Princess Elizabeth reached the age of eighteen, she was at last allowed to 'escape' to join up with the ATS – the Auxiliary Territorial Service – where she became a junior transport officer. Her mother's comment: 'We had sparking plugs all last night at dinner.'

The King had wanted desperately to join the D-Day landings on 6 June 1944, but in the end the idea was vetoed; his chance came when he flew to review the troops in Italy in July. In the meantime, London and the Queen were under attack from doodle-bugs (German flying bombs). She wrote to Queen Mary, 'There is something very inhuman about death-dealing missiles being launched in such an indiscriminate manner.'

VE Day, Victory in Europe, came on 8 May 1945. The celebrations were justly ecstatic throughout the British Isles, but none more heartfelt than those outside Buckingham Palace. There, the crowd witnessed a tremendous eight balcony

The King and Queen with their daughters in the water gardens of Royal Lodge, Windsor. The whole family had worked throughout the years creating an interesting and varied garden – July 1944

appearances by the King and Queen, Princesses Elizabeth and Margaret and the Prime Minister, Winston Churchill. That night, the King allowed his daughters to slip out of the Palace to join the celebrations in the street – 'Poor darlings,' he wrote in his diary, 'they never have had any fun.'

VE Day was, eventually, followed by victory in Japan on 15 August 1945. With typical modesty, the King wrote, 'We have only tried to do our duty during these 5½ years.' During the war, the Queen had written to Queen Mary, 'The destruction is so awful and the people so wonderful – they deserve a better world.' There were so many of those 'wonderful people' throughout the British Isles and the Dominions who were to idolize the Queen and the part she played in the Second World War.

'It was when the war was over', Sir David Bowes-Lyon had said, 'that the King and Queen realized that they could never go back to a scheduled life. They thought it over, and they faced up to their changed life. They made the best of it, and did not waste time crying over what might have been.' They were indeed changed – the King was physically and mentally exhausted after the six years of the war, but he had also emerged as the leader, both of the country and in his family. He never wanted to be King nor she Queen Consort, but once they were King and Queen their position gave them considerable pleasure and strength. He had drawn his strength from the Queen, but it was always a 'mutual' partnership. Her sister, Lady (Jean) Elphinstone, said, 'They were so particularly together, they both leant so much on one another.'

The Royal Family enter the City of London for the Thanksgiving Service at St Paul's, 13 May 1945

The Royal Family and Winston Churchill greet the crowds outside Buckingham Palace on VE Day

Her other sister, Lady (Rose) Granville, added, 'The King was a rock to her, indeed all of us. In fundamental things, she leant on him: I have always felt how much the Queen was sustained by him.'

For the Queen, a different brand of courage to that which she showed during the war was required for post-war Britain. The promise of a 'Brave New World' that had swept the Labour Party into power under Clement Attlee was far away. Instead, there were stringent economies and cuts throughout the country – that, of course, included the Royal Family. Shortages were to be expected and borne in wartime, but were unacceptable in peacetime. There was a drab pall over the country, something that was totally alien to the Queen with her love of gaiety and brightness, not only for herself and her family, but for all. What with the many homeless who had lost their houses in the Blitz and the hardship of Service widows and their children, there was new and important work for the Queen. Through her charities, such as the Soldiers', Sailors' & Airmen's Families Association (SSAFA), she brought much comfort and relief.

The old routine of State functions and visits began again for the King and Queen, although on a

Possibly the first meeting of Princess Elizabeth and Prince Philip of Greece (left), during a visit to the Royal Naval College, Dartmouth, in 1939

very different footing to pre-war. The war had made the King and Queen more approachable – for example, at a garden party at Buckingham Palace for those who had worked for the National Savings scheme, they were virtually mobbed by the enthusiastic crowd, something unthinkable before 1939. The King declared that he had 'never enjoyed anything more', which he would certainly not have done six years earlier. There were also the victory tours of Britain and, ten months after VJ (Victory over Japan) Day, the Victory Parade itself.

The Queen set about restoring her home and family. Slowly Buckingham Palace returned to its former glory – pictures were rehung, steel doors replaced, chandeliers hung and the windows opened up again. She also set about making up for the lost war years with her daughters. There were outings, such as the one with Queen Mary to Covent Garden to see the ballet, *The Sleeping Beauty*, and the King took them to other theatres. There were small, informal 'gramophone' dances held at Buckingham Palace and Royal Lodge for the Princesses, where they met what Queen Mary was to call 'The Body Guard' – invariably Brigade of Guards officers. But Princess Elizabeth had already met the man she wanted to marry.

In 1939 the Princesses accompanied their parents on a visit to the Royal Naval College, Dartmouth, where they were entertained by the young Prince Philip of Greece. As a great-great-grandson of Queen Victoria, he was therefore a cousin of the

Royal Lodge, Windsor, 8 July 1946. Princess Elizabeth strokes Chin, her Tibetan Lion dog

young Princesses and was made welcome at Windsor Castle during the war when he was on leave.

After the war he became a frequent visitor to Buckingham Palace and to Balmoral and it was patently clear that Elizabeth and Philip were in love. He proposed to her in the summer of 1946, she accepted him, and then went to tell her parents. The King considered she was too young to marry, or even to announce her engagement, his judgment possibly clouded by the fact that he was intensely protective of his wife and daughters and the desire to keep his family together. The Queen, on the other hand, saw the marriage to Philip, whom she greatly liked, as an *extension* rather than a threat to their happy family life and gave it her blessing. But the announcement was delayed.

Another reason for delaying the announcement of the engagement may have been the three-month State Visit to South Africa, planned for February 1947. Leaving behind a monstrously cold winter (the King felt guilty at escaping to the sun), the Royal party sailed for Cape Town.

After their tremendous welcome, they set off in the 'White Train' on a 10,000-mile journey which took them through the sheep country of the North-East Cape and the grasslands of the Orange Free State, and on a tour to Basutoland; to Durban; as far north as the Kruger National Park in the Transvaal; to South Africa's other capital of Pretoria; and to Johannesburg and the Rand. The train stopped every two hours for water. Lady Margaret Egerton, one of the Princesses' ladies-in-waiting, remarked on the 'amazing stamina' of the Royal Family, 'They never could be sure of even a quiet meal on the train. Whenever the train stops for cooling or water, crowds of blacks or whites would be there to greet them. Out would come the King and Queen, followed by the Princesses, onto the observation platform, whether they were in the middle of a meal or not.'

The tour was considered a tremendous success, even the Boers being charmed by the Queen and her family. Field-Marshal Jan Smuts believed that thoughts of republicanism had gone forever, yet South Africa was to remain part of the Commonwealth for only another thirteen years. They returned to England with the excitement of

Above *Mother and daughter at Royal Lodge, July 1946 – the summer Prince Philip proposed to the Princess.* Below *The announcement was delayed until after the Royal Tour of South Africa in February 1947*

Princess Elizabeth's engagement to look forward to, but also to the deteriorating health of the King, which, so far, only the Queen had noticed.

Finally, on 10 July 1947, the persistent rumours of the engagement were confirmed with the announcement in the Court Circular:

> It is with the greatest pleasure that the King and Queen announce the betrothal of their dearly beloved daughter, the Princess Elizabeth, to Lieutenant Philip Mountbatten, R.N., son of the late Prince Andrew and the Princess Andrew, to which union the King has gladly given his consent.

The Royal wedding was exactly what was needed to brighten a still drab Britain. In his address, the Archbishop of Canterbury was to emphasize that it was like any other 'cottage' wedding in the country, and, like any other wedding, most of the plans devolved on the bride's mother, the Queen. It was the Queen who organized Norman Hartnell to make the wedding dress and the bridesmaids' dresses and it was she who made those many decisions that have to be made before every wedding. The next day the *Daily Express* reported, 'It was the Queen's personality that shaped the entire wedding.'

Just before the wedding, the King wrote to his daughter:

> Our family, us four, the Royal Family, must remain together, with additions of course at suitable moments!!
>
> I have watched you grow up all these years with pride under the skilful direction of Mummy who, as you know, is the most marvellous person in the world in my eyes and I can, I know, always count on you, and now Philip, to help us in our work.

The wedding, on 20 November 1947, in Westminster Abbey, was a happy, family wedding and, at the same time, exactly what the country expected of a Royal marriage. *Country Life* magazine reported:

> The crowd was enormous, nothing like it had been seen in London since the Coronation ten years ago. And it was a happy, good-tempered crowd obviously determined to enjoy its brief escape from what we have come to call austerity.

The surviving comment of the Queen's thoughts was simply, 'What a wonderful day it has been. They grow up and leave us, and we must make the best of it.'

The country was to have another Royal 'treat' in the celebrations to mark the King and Queen's Silver Wedding on 26 April 1948. There was a service in St Paul's Cathedral attended by friends, relations and dignitaries. The King and Queen were cheered every inch of the way to the Abbey, on their return to Buckingham Palace and on their drive around London, later in the day.

That night they made a broadcast, when the King spoke of their marriage and the comfort he had always found at home. The Queen added:

> I, too, am thankful for our twenty-five years of happiness together, for the opportunities we have been given for service to our beloved country and for the blessings of our home and children. The world of our day is longing to find the secret of community, and all married lives are, in a sense, communities in miniature. Looking back over the last twenty-five years and to my own happy childhood I realize more and more the wonderful sense of security and happiness which comes from a loved home.

Below *A portrait to mark the King and Queen's twenty-fifth wedding anniversary, April 1948.*
Opposite *The Royal Family and Prince Philip of Greece in July 1947 – a family group taken to mark the engagement of Princess Elizabeth and Prince Philip*

The King and Queen were both modestly astounded at the response to their Silver Wedding. Referring to the letters from 'all and sundry thanking us for what we have tried to do during these years', the King wrote to Queen Mary, 'It does spur us on to further efforts.' But those 'other efforts' were to be curtailed all too soon.

The excitement of the news that Princess Elizabeth was expecting her first baby in November was somewhat overshadowed by the King's ill-health. The Queen went to great lengths to keep the seriousness of the King's illness from her daughter and divided her time between the two, taking on many of his engagements – 'It was in character that she should carry on. She would never consider a personal anxiety a reason for not undertaking any duty.' While his grandfather lay ill, Prince Charles Philip Arthur George was born on 14 November 1948, a baby that was to give lasting delight to both grandparents.

The King was only fifty-two and the strain of the war years had left its mark. Like his father, he was a heavy smoker. He had contracted a condition called Buerger's disease, in lay terms a 'severe degeneration of the arteries of the legs' – he had often complained of cramp in his legs. After the experts had conferred, they told him of the obstruction in the circulation of his right leg and that his foot might have to be amputated.

The King's doctors forced him to rest and to cancel the planned tour of Australia and New Zealand, which he did with 'profound regret and bitter disappointment'. Once again, the Queen stepped in and filled the breach at home, cheerfully, despite her personal anguish over the King's condition. Once she told an audience that she was 'the person who once prayed to be granted not a lighter load, but a stronger back'. In March, the doctors decided that they had to operate to save the King's leg, and, with rest and the Queen's

Opposite Still showing signs of strain after the war, the King and Queen photographed at Buckingham Palace. Below Queen Elizabeth holds her grandchild, Prince Charles, at his christening at Buckingham Palace on 15 December 1948

Below In October 1950 the King and Queen's second grandchild, Princess Anne, was christened. Sponsors included Earl Mountbatten, Prince Philip's sister and Queen Elizabeth's nephew while Princess Alice (seated left) stood proxy

unfailing cheerfulness and support, he began to recover slowly. By the August of the next year, 1950, the King felt well enough to consider an Australian Tour in 1952. It was hoped that the second grandchild, Princess Anne, would be born on the Queen's birthday, 4 August, but she arrived eleven days later, 15 August 1950. *The Times* published a birthday tribute to the Queen:

> It would be impossible to overestimate the reinforcement the King has derived from the serene and steady support of the Queen. She has sustained him in sickness and in health, at all times taking her full share of the burdens of royal service and in the time of great anxiety during the King's grave illness, piling new duties upon her already overcrowded programme. . . .

One of the Queen's favourite photographs – her parents with her children on Prince Charles' third birthday

She would commend to all what she told the University of Cape Town were the four cardinal virtues of academic life: honesty, courage, justice and resolve, the whole sustained upon the simplicities and profundities of faith.

During the next year, the King's health fluctuated. The King and Queen attended the opening of the Festival of Britain in 1951, but he was not well enough to receive the King of Norway on his State Visit nor to go to Northern Ireland. On both occasions, the Queen deputized for him. He felt well enough to go to Balmoral, but ended the holiday with a sore throat. As the doctors feared, his condition had worsened, and samples of the King's lung tissue were taken. The Queen learned that he had cancer but kept the diagnosis from her husband. In September, the King had his left lung removed and made a steady recovery. The Queen knew that it was only a matter of time, but her

The King and Queen en route *for Christmas at Sandringham, December 1951. The Queen did much to support her husband after the removal of his left lung*

The three Queens mourn at the King's funeral on 11 February 1952 – Queen Elizabeth II, Queen Mary and Queen Elizabeth the Queen Mother

tremendous courage, fortitude and faith kept her going. There was the usual family Christmas at Sandringham, where the King briefed Princess Elizabeth and the Duke of Edinburgh on the tour of Australia and New Zealand, as they were deputizing for him. On 31 January 1952, they left for East Africa on the first stage of the tour. The King went to see them off at Heathrow, standing on the tarmac in the bitter cold. But then he returned to Sandringham to spend more time recovering in the country air on his Norfolk estate.

The morning of 5 February was dry, cold and sunny. The King was in good spirits and was looking forward to the annual hare-shoot. He shot consistently well all day and greatly enjoyed the company of friends, neighbours, Household and staff. In the evening, he sent a special message of thanks to the keepers, then went out to see one of his labradors that had injured its foot that day. It was his last act, for the 'Squire of Sandringham' died in his sleep early the next morning. His

daughter, far away in a Kenyan wildlife reserve, was now Queen.

'I never knew a woman could be so brave,' the member of the Household who had to break the news to Queen Elizabeth (the Queen Mother) wrote to his wife. In her intense loss and suffering, the Queen Mother calmly sat down and wrote to those close to the late King. She 'told them that she and they must feel gratitude for what had been, rather than distress for what had been lost'. She was still able to give comfort and strength to her family to bear their own inevitably public grief.

Shortly after the funeral, she issued a personal statement which included the paragraph:

Throughout our married life we have tried, the King and I, to fulfil with all our hearts and all our strength the great task of service that was laid upon us. My only wish now is that I may be allowed to continue the work that we sought to do together.

CHAPTER SEVEN

Queen Mother

The Queen Mother once found some lines by William Blake in an annual report of the North Islington Infant Welfare Centre, of which she is patron, and has quoted them often:

Labour well the minute particulars, attend to the little ones,
And those who are in misery cannot remain so, long.

She recalled them that fateful morning of 6 February 1952, as she played with her young grandchildren, Charles and Anne – 'I have got to start sometime, and it is better now than later.' From that noble 'start', the Queen Mother has never stopped loving, caring and working for her family, the monarchy and, not least, for everybody else, wherever they come from.

Initially, such service outside her family was done through the memory of the late King. A friend revealed that 'Her daughters were wonderful with Queen Elizabeth during that dreadful time, but her guiding beacon in her loneliness has been what her husband would have wished her to do. Throughout her terrible sorrow and sadness, Queen Elizabeth has made a great effort to remake her life. Everything she has done as a widow is because she knows the King would like her to do it.' A very private visit from Winston Churchill at Birkhall may also have had much to do with the Queen Mother's brave emergence into public life.

She met the challenge head on. Only three months after the death of the King, and not feeling well, the Queen Mother flew up to Scotland to see

Above *Always beautifully dressed, the Queen Mother wears a favourite diamond brooch.* Right *The young Prince Charles leads his grandmother and mother to the stands at the Guards Polo Club in Windsor Park*

The Queen Mother with Princess Margaret attends the Queen's first Trooping the Colour, 5 June 1952

The Queen Mother with Honey at the Castle of Mey in October 1955 – it had taken three years to renovate

the First Battalion of the Black Watch before they left for active service in Korea. Totally composed, their Colonel-in-Chief inspected the guard of honour and spoke to the officers and men. The visit had a wider meaning than the pleasure it gave that Highland Regiment, it proved to the Queen Mother that she could carry on on her own. When a friend was later to comment on how brave she was, the Queen Mother replied, 'Not when I am alone.'

She set about gathering together the Household of a Queen Mother – a Lord Chamberlain, a comptroller, secretaries, equerries, ladies-in-waiting – all employed by her, but all great personal friends. They refer to Queen Elizabeth II as 'The Queen' and the Queen Mother as 'Queen Elizabeth'.

Not long after the King's death, the Queen Mother went to stay with her great friends Commander Clare and Lady Doris Vyner at their home, 'The House of the Northern Gate' – the most northerly house on mainland Scotland. There, she heard of a castle that had failed to sell at auction. Immediately, she went to see Barrogill, overlooking the Pentland Firth, the home of the Earls of

Caithness. When she heard that it was likely to be pulled down, she replied, 'Pull it down? Never! I'll buy it.' Once the castle was hers, she gave it the old name of the Castle of Mey and began to restore both it and the gardens. It was a long, and expensive, project, but it did provide the Queen Mother with a new and exciting outside interest, as well as the first home that she had ever owned in her own right. With her infinite flare, she made it warm and 'cosy', but at the same time kept the character of the castle. It is a place, with its wildness and striking views towards the Orkneys, that became a great comfort to the Queen Mother in those first years of widowhood. Later, it was to become more than that, with a small hill farm and a herd of Aberdeen Angus cattle, a prize flock of sheep, a market garden and the delights of her neighbours' fishing on the Thurso River.

The Castle of Mey was not the only new home for the Queen Mother. The Buckingham Palace that she had been so reluctant to move into now had such fond memories of her husband that she

Clarence House, London

was reluctant to move out. The Queen and the Duke of Edinburgh moved into the Belgium Suite from Clarence House while 'the Clarence', as it is affectionately known, was being renovated for the Queen Mother. Ever mindful of her staff, she had insisted that their quarters were fully modernized in the plans too. It was finally finished two weeks before the Coronation in May 1953. Balmoral was less of a wrench to leave as she returned to Birkhall, the house that George V had given them as Duke and Duchess of York. Never still for a moment, she later had a wing, with six bedrooms, built for her guests. Of course, Royal Lodge has remained the favourite of all her residences.

There was to be a further tragedy soon in her life – the death of the venerable Queen Mary, just three months before the Coronation. For all the time she had known her, Queen Mary had remained a stalwart pillar of the monarchy and a constant example and friend of the Queen Mother. She was to miss her deeply. There was to be another great upheaval to her life that broke just before the Coronation – Princess Margaret told her that she wished to marry Group Captain Peter Townsend, a recently divorced man. Townsend, a brave and good-looking fighter pilot, had been appointed equerry to the King in 1944 (when Princess Margaret was fourteen) and had later become the Comptroller of the Queen Mother's Household. When Townsend informed the Queen Mother (repeated in his memoirs), she 'listened with characteristic understanding . . . without a sign that she felt angered or outraged – or that she acquiesced – and the Queen Mother was never anything but considerate in her attitude to me. She never once hurt either of us throughout the

The Queen Mother watches with Prince Charles and Princess Margaret at Queen Elizabeth II's Coronation in May 1953

Another crisis in the family – Princess Margaret announced in 1953 that she wished to marry Group Captain Peter Townsend, seen here in South Africa

Queen Elizabeth the Queen Mother, 1953 – a portrait by Cecil Beaton, another of the talented photographers used by the Royal Family

whole difficult affair'. Only the Queen Mother knows how much the affair hurt her.

Princess Margaret would undoubtedly have been given the consent of the Privy Council to marry Peter Townsend had he not been divorced, but, as all descendants of George II in the line of succession need the consent of the Privy Council to marry if under twenty-five, and Princess Margaret was rising twenty-three, it would not have been granted. However, it was not put to the test, then or later.

The Coronation of her daughter on 2 June 1953 brought back many happy and poignant memories of the Queen Mother's own Coronation just sixteen years before, a deeply religious and symbolic occasion. The tradition that the dowager queen did not attend the next Coronation had been broken by Queen Mary in 1937 and the Queen Mother was a vital part of her daughter's great occasion. In the procession, she cannot have failed to have been warmed by the crowd's involuntary

cheer. The *Daily Express* correspondent did not miss her entrance in the Abbey. 'On she came up the aisle with a bow here to Prince Bernhard, a bow there to the row of Ambassadors, and up those tricky steps with no looking down' – something she learned from her mother. 'She is the only woman I ever saw who can slow up naturally when she sees a camera.'

Another camera 'that saw' at the Coronation was the one that picked up Princess Margaret removing a piece of fluff from Peter Townsend's uniform as they laughed together in the Great Hall of Westminster Abbey. It was patently obvious, even from the press photograph, that they were in love. The 'story' broke twelve days later. While mother and sister were fiercely loyal to a much-loved daughter and sister, and wished to protect her from the public outcry and to promote her happiness, they were also staunch upholders of the teachings of the Church of England, the Queen being the Defender of the Faith. Shades of 'for the woman

An informal picture of the Queen Mother with her favourite grandson, Prince Charles, and Pippin at Royal Lodge, Windsor, on 7 April 1954

I love' and memories of the nightmare of the Abdication returned to the Queen Mother. However, it was Winston Churchill who came up with the best solution. Townsend should leave the Queen Mother's Household for two years (he was sent to Brussels as Air Attaché), for by the end of that time Princess Margaret could marry whom she pleased. 'They gave us hope,' the Princess said.

The tour of Southern Rhodesia, now Zimbabwe, to mark the centenary of the birth of Cecil Rhodes, her first overseas visit without her husband, was to be a great test for the Queen Mother. Believing that travel is a panacea to all troubles, she asked Princess Margaret to join her.

The tour was a great success, although Princess Margaret caught a severe chill. The stamina of the Queen Mother and her inherent interest in all whom she met, had not deserted her in widowhood.

When the Queen and the Duke of Edinburgh went on their promised Commonwealth tour in 1953, the Queen Mother took up her former role, taking care of her grandchildren and, as the senior Councillor of State, deputizing for the Queen.

The invitation in 1954 to visit the United States, with a few days in Canada, was a daunting prospect for the Queen Mother. She did not believe that the Americans would turn out to see 'a middle-aged lady, and a widow at that'. She sailed on the *Queen Elizabeth*, the liner named after her and launched by her just before the war. She told the welcoming committee that she was 'delighted to find myself once again in New York and among its kind and friendly people'. The kind people of New York were merely civil when she drove to her two major functions – to receive an honorary doctorate from Columbia University and to receive a substantial cheque for the King George VI Memorial fund, money to sponsor Commonwealth students in the United States. She was so nervous at the official dinner at the Waldorf-Astoria Hotel, with the television cameras on her the whole time, that she could not eat anything. Afterwards, when she returned to her hosts, Sir Pierson and Lady Dixon, she was asked if there was anything she would like, to which she replied that she would love some scrambled eggs. 'The supper was served on trays in the drawing room: Queen Elizabeth [the Queen Mother], in tremendous form, took off her tiara and, laying it on the sofa beside her, ate supper from a tray in a lively picnic atmosphere.'

Suddenly, the Queen Mother began 'to take off'. At every function there was more enthusiasm, greater media coverage. The charisma which the Queen Mother had thought had died with her husband was very much 'alive and well' and working in New York. When she tried to go shopping in Saks, the fashionable store on Fifth Avenue, she was besieged. She moved on to Washington to stay with the President and Mrs Eisenhower at the White House before paying a short visit to Canada's capital, Ottawa, and then returning to New York. When she departed for England, she left behind a captivated and positively pro-British America. One New Yorker wrote, 'In the Queen Mother, Americans discovered to their delight, warmth, sincerity, frankness, democratic bearing, interest in American Institutions and a vigour that no one imagined that a Queen could have.' To the Americans, she was 'Ma Queen' (from a New York taxi driver) or the 'Queen Mom' and in Canada she was dubbed the 'Queen Mum' – the soubriquet that, fortunately, was the one to stick.

One of the most important honours that the Queen Mother has accepted is that of Chancellor of London University. It was important for the University, who gained a tireless and dedicated Chancellor, it was important for the Queen Mother, who gained a totally new and outside interest and a cause to work for. As her Private Secretary, Sir Martin Gilliat, said, 'It was the spark that set off this tumultuously varied way of life.' Twenty years later, she was to address the Founder's

Day Dinner, 'I see they [the former Chancellors] all retire at seventy-five. I've enjoyed it so much.' She sat down, then rose to her feet and continued, 'I've decided to carry on.' Her parting present was kept for five years until she retired in 1980. To her great pleasure, her granddaughter, Princess Anne, was voted in in her place. When she left, she had 'clocked' up over three hundred separate visits to, and connected with, the University, an average of over twelve a year.

The agony of what was to be dubbed 'the Townsend affair' loomed up again on Princess Margaret's twenty-fifth birthday. He returned to London in October only to find there was a phrase in the Marriage Act that had been overlooked – that Princess Margaret could marry 'except that both Houses of Parliament shall declare their disapprobation thereto'. Anthony Eden, the new Prime Minister, had to inform the Queen that the majority of Parliament would not sanction the marriage. The only way out would be for Princess Margaret to renounce her royal position. The Queen Mother could not help her daughter make

In October 1954 the Queen Mother was invited to visit North America – at the Observation Tower of the Empire State Building, New York

the decision between her happiness with the man she loved, which cut across her deep religious faith, and her duty. Finally, Princess Margaret issued the statement that she would not marry Group Captain Peter Townsend, 'but, mindful of the Church's teaching that marriage is indissoluble, and conscious of my duty to the Commonwealth, I have resolved to put these considerations before others. . . .' It is a sad postscript that twenty years later when Princess Margaret filed for divorce from Lord Snowdon, there was not a murmur from the Church. Their position had not changed, only the times.

The Queen Mother was not 'allowed' to stay still or in one place for long. She was, of course, a natural choice to open the Franco-Scottish exhibition in Paris in the spring of 1956. As in the summer of 1938, she captivated them all, with her speech in flawless French, which began: 'Being Scots, I love France as all my countrymen have done.' Nothing would come between the Queen Mother and her engagements. However, they can often be arranged so that they do not clash with one of her principal, private passions, the love of steeplechasing. The

One of the National Hunt's favourite patrons – the Queen Mother with her horse, Devon Loch, at Sandown, 1956

Queen Mother was back from France in plenty of time for the Grand National at Aintree, where her highly fancied, and favourite horse, Devon Loch, had been entered for the famous race.

The Queen Mother's interest in racing began in 1949, when her friend, the great amateur jockey Lord (Anthony) Mildmay, suggested that she become an owner. She shared her first horse, named Montaveen, with her daughter, Princess Elizabeth. The Irish-bred horse was sent to Peter Cazalet to train. Montaveen won his first race in Princess Elizabeth's colours at Fontwell Park and went on to win again before breaking a leg at Hurst Park, when he had to be destroyed. Her next horse, Manicou, was owned outright and raced in the Queen Mother's colours – light blue, buff stripes, blue sleeves, black cap and gold tassle, the colours of her amateur jockey great-uncle, the 12th Earl of Strathmore. The horse that has been inextricably linked with the Queen Mother is Devon Loch, a good-looking, strongly built, dark bay horse, 16.2 hands high. His jockey, Dick Francis (now a thriller writer), was to declare that 'he had a hell of a feel' about him and that he would make the Grand National. He was right. In 1956 the Queen Mother went up to Aintree and spent the night on the Royal Train; next morning she saw her horses riding out. Dick Francis wrote in his autobiography, *Sport of Queens*, 'Usually the National is more of a worry than a pleasure to anyone riding in it: Devon Loch made it a delight. . . .' On the run in, just ten strides from the winning post, disaster struck. For some inexplicable reason (possibly the crescendo of the crowd cheering a popular Royal winner of the greatest steeplechase in the world), Devon Loch was down, his back legs stiffened and he was overtaken by E.S.B. The Queen Mother 'never turned a hair', but said, 'I must go down and comfort those poor people.' The distraught Francis was told, 'Please don't be upset . . . that's racing.'

Every year, the Queen Mother would stay with the Cazalets at Fairlawne for their local meeting at Lingfield Park. The stable staff loved her visits, the head lad, Jim Fairgrieve, remembering that on '. . . Saturday morning, Her Majesty would be on the gallops watching the horses work. It was great to watch her in her Wellington boots and headscarf, an icy wind blowing, sometimes a sleety

Derby Day 1983 – the Queen Mother in the paddock at Epsom Racecourse

shower. Her head would be up facing the gallop and enjoying every minute of it. . . .' It was rewarding for the Queen Mother, and the loyal stable at Fairlawne, that she should have had her first treble, three winners in a day, at Lingfield with Laffy, Double Star and The Rip – the latter being bred near Sandringham at the Red Cat Hotel from her favourite, Manicou. The 1960s were particularly successful for the Queen Mother, but, once again, tragedy struck with the death of her dear friend and trainer Peter Cazalet. He trained over 1,100 winners, nearly a quarter of them for his Royal owner. The yard was disbanded and most of the Queen Mother's horses went to Fulke Walwyn at Lambourne. Today, she has fewer horses in training and less success, although at the end of the 1984 season she had won 351 races to date. Her greatest victory came at the end of that season when she won the Whitbread Gold Cup at Sandown on 28 April 1984. It was a brilliant race and the most

exciting finish when Special Cargo came from an impossible position to win by a short head. The telephone in the Royal Box rang ceaselessly as the Queen, the Prince of Wales, Princess Anne and Prince Andrew all congratulated her.

She is dearly loved by the racing world – who else would go on a miserable day to see a new horse run in a novice hurdle-race at a minor race-meeting far from the warmth of the home fire? The Injured Jockeys' Fund also knows what it is like to have her as patron, as do countless numbers of stable lads, jockeys and trainers who have received a letter or some gift from her. The 'punters' are deeply loyal to her as well – 'If there is a shorter cut', said one of them, 'to a bloody nose in Tattersalls than to criticize the Queen Mother in any way, I don't know it.'

If the Queen dismissed the suggestion that the Queen Mother should become GG, Governor-General, of Canada or Australia with, 'We can't do without her', she at least gave her blessing for her mother to accept the flood of invitations to all Commonwealth countries. In the summer of 1957

A portrait to mark the Queen Mother's departure for her tour of Rhodesia and Nyasaland in June 1957

she visited Rhodesia and Nyasaland, now Zimbabwe, Zambia and Malawi. In her role of 'mother', she was dubbed *Mambo Kazi*, 'Big Mother' – a reference to her importance. She was installed as President of the University, opened the King George VI Memorial Hospital for Handicapped Children and even went below ground in a copper mine. Characteristically, she was more interested in meeting people than seeing machinery. It was on that tour that one of her equerries left his brief-case behind and with it the Queen Mother's next speech. Between engagements on the aeroplane, the speech was hastily rewritten. It was delivered, and as the Queen Mother handed the paper back to the equerry, she said with a twinkle, 'I think we did that rather nicely, didn't we?' The 'we' was not 'the Royal we', the Queen Mother thinks of her Household as an extension of her family.

Demands were made on the Queen Mother the next year to make another visit to Australia and

During the tour of Australia the Queen Mother nurses a koala bear at Queensland University, February 1958

New Zealand. That tour was to be the first round-the-world flight for any member of the Royal Family. It was a phenomenal flight – she landed in Montreal in a snowstorm and Vancouver in a downpour, then, after a day's rest, a touchdown in Honolulu, then on across the Pacific to Fiji, where she had to down a bowl of *kava*, the same local drink that her husband had protected her from on her last visit. Another short rest, then on to Auckland, New Zealand – nearly four days in the air with three night stops. In New Zealand, she managed to tour both the North and the South Island, this time taking her doctor's advice by resting. The same warm New Zealand welcome greeted her, and the Prime Minister, Mr Keith Holyoake, spoke for the country when he said, 'It's tremendous! She's terrific! There are no adjectives left to do justice to this tour. It is simply amazing to think what she has achieved in two weeks, not only in spreading happiness wherever she goes, but in strengthening – as she has said herself – the bonds that tie us to the Mother country.' With a sweep of the hand, he continued, 'Look at all these people, she has done something wonderful for them.'

The New Zealand Prime Minister could have been talking for the people of Australia too. Originally, she was to visit only the eastern states, but, again, she took in most of the continent. The weather was extreme, but the Queen Mother soldiered on with her characteristic smile, 'I enjoyed it all.' She also enjoyed the more informal approach to the whole tour, where she could meet more people to talk to, rather than driving past, all too quickly for her liking. An organizer of the tour recalled that 'as it was Queen Elizabeth's wish . . . we were able to do a lot more to make it a fact'. At times, it was almost too much. Her aides would have to link arms to protect her from over-enthusiastic crowds. 'But I've come a thousand miles to see her,' they would cry. 'You won't see her by laying her out,' came the patient reply. A member of the Household remembered that 'it was her own personality that made it . . . she aroused devotion – devotion from those who served her and those who saw her . . . we did feel that she was enjoying it'. It is a very special person that can enjoy a sixteen-hour day with fifteen different engagements.

The bad luck that dogged her last return from Australia in HMS *Renown* was with her for the flight back to London via Mauritius, Nairobi and

Malta. When approaching Mauritius, one of the engines seized. Typically, the Queen Mother was not in the least concerned, or if she was she did not show it. The aeroplane landed on three engines, but it was days before a replacement was fitted. Short of time, the visit to Nairobi was cut out (she was to return to Kenya the following year, where she was dubbed the Rainmaker when her visit coincided with the end of the drought) and the aeroplane landed at Entebbe, Uganda. There, another fault was found and another day lost before flying on to Malta, where a hydraulic fault was located. Finally, the Queen Mother abandoned her QANTAS flight and returned home in another aeroplane, nearly three days late.

The first published photographs of the baby Prince Andrew were taken with his grandmother on her sixtieth birthday with his brother and sister, August 1960

Sixty is the legal age for retirement for women in Britain, but, in the Queen Mother's sixtieth year, she was as busy and active as usual. It was also a happy year. She saw Princess Margaret married to the photographer Anthony Armstrong-Jones, who was created the Earl of Snowdon on his marriage. She was also off on another overseas tour, again to the Federation of Rhodesia and to Nyasaland to open the Kariba dam.

It was during this tour that the New York *Daily News* ludicrously published the story that the Queen Mother was about to marry again. Her treasurer, then aged seventy-four, Sir Arthur Penn, was named as the 'bridegroom'. On this rare occasion, the Queen Mother was very annoyed and instructed her press officer to refute the extraordinary story as 'complete and absolute rubbish'. The press officer added ruefully that 'in fact Her Majesty used a stronger word'.

For her sixtieth birthday, the Queen Mother had the added pleasure of being photographed with her third grandchild, the six-month-old Prince Andrew, born on 19 February. She spent the day quietly, lunching with Princess Margaret and the Queen, before flying north to the Castle of Mey.

That next year was no less taxing. Despite breaking a bone in her foot after an accident at Royal Lodge, she carried on her multifarious engagements, such as the launching of the liner *Northern Star*. Later in the year she was off overseas again, to Tunisia. The use of the Royal Yacht *Britannia* made the travelling so much easier and far less of a strain. The following year, when she went to Canada, she flew on an ordinary commercial flight to Ottawa for the centenary of the Black Watch (Royal Highland Regiment) of Canada among many other engagements.

Not all the Queen Mother's trips abroad were official. She had long had a close affinity for France and, at the suggestion of Sir Pierson Dixon, the then British Ambassador, she went there for a holiday. She took over a floor of a hotel, the Château du Puits d'Artigny at Montbazon, south of Tours in the Loire valley, with her friends (the party included Lady Fermoy, grandmother of the present Princess of Wales) and from there made daily sorties to the châteaux of the Loire. She has returned to France many times since for short holidays, taking a small house in the Burgundy country. An avid sightseer, there can never be too many châteaux, gardens or churches to visit.

Another tour of Australia and New Zealand and Canada scheduled for 1964 had to be postponed when the Queen Mother entered the King Edward VII Hospital, where she had her appendix removed in a thirty-minute operation. It was difficult for her doctors to persuade her that the tour should be cancelled and that it was essential she should have a complete rest. Instead, she went in the Royal Yacht *Britannia* for a cruise in the Caribbean with family and friends. Before she left, she was able to see her latest grandchild, Prince Edward, born on 10 March. She was to return to the West Indies the following year, when she visited the University of the West Indies in Jamaica. She visited Canada again, ostensibly on a private visit – but what visit can be private where the Queen Mother is concerned?

The revived tour of Australia and New Zealand in 1966 also happily coincided with her favourite grandson's, the Prince of Wales, time at the Geelong Church of England Grammar School, Timbertop, in the State of Victoria. They met up and spent a magical weekend in a cottage in the Snowy Mountains, fishing in the River Bend. After her sixteen-day tour, the Queen Mother sailed on in the Royal Yacht to spend Easter in Fiji, where, inexplicably, the islanders broke with their custom of remaining silent in the presence of Royalty and warmly cheered the Queen Mother. She then returned to New Zealand, where she encountered some anti-monarchist demonstrators and retraced old, familiar and loved ground. She also managed to squeeze in a little trout fishing in the North Island. After only catching a two-pound trout, she was heard to mutter, 'It would be better to get one out of the deep freeze!'

The stamina of the Queen Mother seemed to be inexhaustible, but even she had her relapses. On her return from New Zealand, she entered the King Edward VII Hospital again, this time for a check-up. When she returned in December, it was to stay for a 'little while' – that little while being Christmas until just before the New Year. The

A portrait study taken for Her Majesty's sixty-third birthday – in the Drawing Room at Clarence House

Royal surgeons operated, amid much concern from the public. The final bulletin announced that the Queen Mother 'had undergone an operation to relieve a partial obstruction of the abdomen'. This announcement launched a flood of letters, telegrams and cards to Clarence House, with mountains of flowers. They showed that the nation really cared. A nice treat was laid on for her by Peter Cazalet, 'the Führer' as she called him, when he arranged for all her horses to be paraded before her at Clarence House.

It was not long before the Queen Mother was back 'in harness' again. In 1967 there were two trips abroad – a trip to France to the Normandy beaches on the twenty-third anniversary of the Allied Invasion and one to Canada to the Eastern Provinces in Royal Yacht *Britannia*. From this point on, the Queen Mother began to ease up on her overseas travel. It will be a long time, however, before any member of the Royal Family can match her record for travel. She has known every form of transport, from battle cruiser to Concorde (in which she flew to Iran as guest of the Shah in 1975). In all these years she has shown that she cares and her smiling face has been seen by millions around the world. To her, it is not a job – it is, to use her favourite expression, 'such fun!'

Where the 1950s and 1960s for the Queen Mother were marked with her highly acclaimed overseas tours, the 1970s and 1980s have been marked with family milestones that have been celebrated with pomp and pageantry, and thus shared, not just with the people of Britain but, via television, with every country in the world. Interspersed with these overseas tours and pageants, the relentless round of public engagements continues as well as the invaluable work that the Queen Mother does 'at home'.

Every year she takes part in Trooping the Colour – a highly ritualistic display on Horse

A time to remember – the Queen Mother watches the Cenotaph ceremony on Remembrance Sunday 1983

The first woman to hold office as Lord Warden of the Cinque Ports, the Queen Mother visits Dover, 1980

The last Queen Consort with the future Queen Consort – Trooping the Colour in June 1981

The Prince of Wales' Investiture at Caernarfon Castle 1969 – a proud moment for the Queen Mother

Guards Parade to mark the Queen's official birthday. Held usually on the second Saturday in June, the Queen Mother rarely fails to be an integral part of the great day as she drives, often with Princess Margaret or one of her grandchildren, in an open landau to Whitehall. There, from a balcony high over the parade ground, she watches the glittering spectacle before returning, invariably to extra cheers from the great crowd as she passes, to Buckingham Palace and the balcony appearances.

Another annual occasion which the Queen Mother never likes to miss is the Remembrance Day Service on the Sunday closest to 11 November. There, high up on the balcony above the Cenotaph, a member of her Household lays a wreath on her behalf. During those poignant moments she, too, remembers those who died in the two world wars, particularly within her family. The Queen Mother usually attends the Royal Ascot Meeting, driving up the course in the traditional parade of Ascot Landaus with members of her family or her house party who stay at Royal Lodge. Also in Ascot Week is the annual Order

of the Garter Service at St George's Chapel within Windsor Castle. The Queen Mother is a Lady of the Garter and never misses, unless she can not possibly help it, the procession and service of the 'Most Noble Order in the land'.

One ancient and moving ceremony that gave particular pleasure to the Queen Mother was the Investiture of her grandson, Prince Charles, as the twenty-first Prince of Wales. He had been created Prince of Wales in 1958, but, as the Queen said in a recorded message, 'When he is grown up, I will present him to you at Caernarfon.' This she did, on 2 July 1969, in a ceremony beautifully 'stage-managed' by Lord Snowdon, Constable of Caernarfon Castle. The Queen Mother watched the ceremony from the side with Princess Anne, Princess Margaret and Lord Snowdon. Four hundred million television viewers around the world also witnessed the wonderful occasion.

The Silver Wedding of the Queen and the Duke of Edinburgh on 20 November 1972 was a fine demonstration of a happy family event that was celebrated by the nation. Even that Number One critic of the monarchy, Willie Hamilton MP, congratulated them in the House of Commons. That night, the Queen rose to her feet, 'I think everyone will concede that today, of all occasions, I should begin my speech with, "My husband and I".' The Queen Mother must surely have thought of her own wedding, nearly seventy years before, and happy marriage, so cruelly cut short.

The Queen's Silver Jubilee was marked with great celebrations and a patriotic show of loyalty to the Crown. While the Queen and the Duke of Edinburgh were on their Antipodean Tour, the Queen Mother stood in as Councillor of State. She who had done so much to uphold and further the cause of the monarchy could now take some credit that the system had not only survived in a changing world but had continued to be loved and revered. But the Queen Mother never takes credit for her own labours. She took great pleasure in driving to the Service of Thanksgiving at St Paul's Cathedral on Jubilee Day, 7 June 1977, with three of her grandsons, the Prince of Wales in the full dress uniform as Colonel of the Welsh Guards and the Princes Andrew and Edward. Hers was a special cheer from the crowd.

An honour that was entirely hers was the installation of the Queen Mother as Constable of Dover Castle and Lord Warden and Admiral of the Cinque Ports in 1979 – the first woman ever to hold the honour. The Queen Mother sailed to Dover for the ceremony in the Royal Yacht *Britannia* and arrived, with two of her grandchildren, Viscount Linley and Lady Sarah Armstrong-Jones, to gun salutes and a full procession with the Household Cavalry. The weather, intermittent downpours and bright sunshine, did not deter her enjoyment as she 'plunged' into the enthusiastic crowds, where she had a special word for the children and those in wheelchairs. The Archbishop of Canterbury spoke for them all when he said in his address, 'We all owe her more than can ever be repaid.'

It was a little under a month later, 27 August 1979, that the Prince of Wales was lunching with the Queen Mother at Birkhall when they heard the tragic news of the death of Lord Mountbatten, 'Uncle Dickie' to the Royal Family, murdered with three others in Ireland when the IRA planted a bomb in his fishing boat. It was a numbing shock for them all. Lord Mountbatten had already planned his own funeral and, for the Royal Family, especially the Queen Mother, who was a contemporary of the Earl, their very private grief was shared publicly at his funeral service.

The occasion that the nation had really been waiting for to demonstrate their love and loyalty to the Queen Mother came with the celebrations for her eightieth birthday. It was a time when all could indulge their very best emotions for her. There was a wonderful ball at Buckingham Palace, which she shared with the Dowager Duchess of Gloucester and the Duke of Beaufort, who were also nearing their eightieth birthdays. All their friends were invited. Although her official birthday is on 4 August, it was decided to hold the very special service of thanksgiving at St Paul's Cathedral a few weeks earlier.

They called it 'Queen's weather'. The rain, which had been falling solidly for two days and threatened to mar the celebrations on 15 July 1980, suddenly stopped that morning. It was undeniably the Queen Mother's day. The Queen and the Duke of Edinburgh and other members of the Royal Family drove to the Cathedral ahead of her so as not to steal any of the thunder of the great octogenarian. The honour of escorting the Queen Mother to St Paul's went to the Prince of Wales. They drove from Buckingham Palace, along The Mall and to the City, up Ludgate Hill to the Cathedral, the crowds standing four deep, cheering all the way. As an extra tribute to her mother, the Queen had ordained that she should be accompanied by the complete Sovereign's Escort of the Household Cavalry – a rare but deserved honour.

As she alighted from the state landau, the crowds could see the Queen Mother. She was all they ever hoped for. She was dressed in a style they had long grown to love – a shimmering of ostrich feathers and violet-blue chiffon with floating panels. Although a cold day, she wore no coat. A fanfare of trumpets heralded her arrival and her procession down the aisle and through the 2,700 personally invited guests. Apart from the Heads of State and ambassadors and representatives from all over the world, there were those personal friends and staff who had served her so loyally over the years – the cook from 145 Piccadilly, her housekeeper from the Castle of Mey and the like.

The service, taken by the Dean of St Paul's, was ecumenical, with the Moderator of the Church of

A summer portrait – the Queen Mother, still a radiant and regal queen, on her eightieth birthday

The Queen Mother's triumphant carriage ride, with Prince Charles as her escort, to the Birthday Service held at St Paul's in honour of her eightieth birthday

An eightieth birthday party for the Queen Mother – a special première performance of Rhapsody *and a party back-stage at the Royal Opera House Covent Garden*

Scotland reading the lesson and Cardinal Hume saying two prayers. The Archbishop of Canterbury, who later described the service as 'the most beautiful I've taken', gave the address. 'It is difficult to fall in love with committees or policies, but the Queen Mother has shown a human face which has called out affection and loyalty and a sense of belonging, without which a nation loses its heart.'

The celebrations were not over for the Queen Mother as there was still her actual birthday to mark. Flowers and tributes from all over the world poured into Clarence House. The band of the Welsh Guards played 'Happy Birthday to You' as they marched down The Mall. As the guns boomed out their salute in Hyde Park and at the Tower of London, the great black, wooden gates swung open and the crowd, most of it children, surged forward to present their flowers and home-made birthday cards. There was a fly-past from the Royal Air Force, who emblazoned the letter 'E' in the sky with vapour trails.

That night, there was a 'treat' for the Queen Mother at Covent Garden, when, in a triple bill of ballet, her old friend Sir Frederick Ashton had choreographed *Rhapsody* which was performed specially for her for its world première. The evening ended with thousands of silver petals showering from the ceiling. But it was not quite the end of the evening for the Queen Mother, who then went 'back-stage' for a party laid on by the Opera House staff. The balloons that floated about bore the message, 'We Love You Queen Mum'. It said it all. For everyone.

It is the dearest wish of the Queen Mother to see everyone, especially her family, happy. She knows only too well the joys that a happy marriage and children can bring, and, unlike some in his family, the Queen Mother never doubted that the Prince of Wales would find in time the right girl to marry, one who would make him happy and help him in his life's work. She never doubted that he could do the same for his wife. As the world knows, he found the Lady Diana Spencer, and his choice gave the Queen Mother an even greater pleasure.

For years, Lady (Ruth) Fermoy had been a close friend of the Queen Mother – they are both Scotswomen and Lady Fermoy had lived at Park House, within the grounds of the Sandringham Estate, for many years. Lady Fermoy has also been the Queen Mother's Woman of the Bedchamber and Lady-in-Waiting; she is now Extra-Lady-in-Waiting. They share the same love of music and Norfolk and were both delighted when her daughter, Frances, married the young Viscount Althorp, heir to the 7th Earl Spencer. The Spencer family have been closely linked to the Queen Mother as Lord Spencer's wife and two sisters, Lady Delia Peel and Lady (Lavinia) Annaly, were all in her Household. The ties of friendship and service were indeed close. The Queen Mother took a keen interest in the Spencer children, particularly after the breakdown of their parents' marriage, when Lady Fermoy stepped in to help her son-in-law.

It must have given the Queen Mother great pleasure when Lady Diana Spencer was asked to stay at Balmoral in the summer of 1979 and was brought over to tea at Birkhall. When it was realized that she was at Balmoral the next year as the guest of the Prince of Wales, the press went wild with speculation. Here, the Queen Mother was able to help – not in the role of 'cupid', there was no need for that, but to offer a safe refuge at Birkhall for them both. She knew the pressures on the young Lady Diana – after her own engagement was announced she said, 'Once the cat is out of the bag, you cannot stuff it back in!' When the engagement was announced, Lady Diana stayed that night with the Queen Mother at Clarence House and remained there for a few days.

Lady Diana Spencer returned to Clarence House to spend the night before the Royal Wedding there. After dinner, the two sat and watched the firework display in Hyde Park on television. There was a dreadful fear that the Queen Mother, who had injured her leg, might not be well

The Queen Mother arrives at St Helier port from HMY Britannia *during her visit to the Channel Islands, 1 June 1984*

enough to attend the wedding, but those who feared did not know the Queen Mother. Nothing would keep her down, that day of all days. She was up early, welcoming her friends and those who had come to attend to the bride. Dressed in her aquamarine silk dress with ostrich feather hat, she left by car for Buckingham Palace. Then she appeared again in the triumphal procession to St Paul's Cathedral, accompanied by Prince Edward, who was acting as his brother's supporter. Her smile and her wave matched the happy day.

On her gilt chair beside the Duke of Edinburgh and the Queen, the Queen Mother had 'pride of place' to see her grandson married. Across the aisle sat Lady Fermoy – two *very* proud grandmothers. After the wedding and the procession back to the Palace came the rapturous balcony appearances, where the Queen Mother had stood so many times before – all of them happy occasions: her own wedding, their return from Australia and New Zealand, their Coronation and the end of the war.

It was no accident that Prince William of Wales was christened William Arthur Philip Louis on 4 August 1982 – the Queen Mother's eighty-second birthday. The Royal Family and godparents gathered in the Music Room of Buckingham Palace, where the Archbishop of Canterbury

A special family occasion – Prince William's christening 1982 was held on his great-grandmother's birthday

performed the service. When the Queen Mother took her great-grandson in her arms, he started to bawl, to which she replied, 'Quite right. He's wanting lunch. He's made his first public speech and he's got good lungs.' That day, seated on the sofa was the span of three centuries – the Queen Mother, born in the reign of Queen Victoria, and in her arms the King of England in the twenty-first century.